9-28-61

Life with Women

and

How to Survive it

BY THE SAME AUTHOR

ALL ABOUT MEN
WHAT NEXT, DOCTOR PECK?

Life with Women

and

How to Survive it

Joseph H. Peck, M.D.

Illustrated by

Eric Gurney

PRENTICE-HALL, INC.

Englewood Cliffs, N. J.

Third printing . . . . *September, 1961*

© 1961 by Prentice-Hall, Inc.

Library of Congress Catalog Card Number: 61-8072

Printed in the United States of America

53663-T

1159971

Dedicated to the memory of Marg Rydalch and Eliza Bowen—
two grand old Utah women whose lives were spent in service
to "the least of these" as their God commanded.

Table of Contents

Table of Contents

Preface
A LITTLE BATTING PRACTICE

This book is written for the average man who has neither the time nor the inclination to read the women's magazines or the findings of noted psychiatrists, anthropologists and the like on the subject of the female and the vagaries of her mentality and deportment. I have not read all this literature, otherwise I would be nuttier than I am. But in the preparation of this handy guide to ruin, in addition to the experience of seventy-five years association with women, I have waded through some mighty queer books by lady experts. I have even ventured into cocktail bars (properly chaperoned by my wife, of course) to watch these curious animals as they relaxed. It is said that one will do anything for his art, and so I am not ashamed to confess that I have also gone so far as to speak to groups of women, trying to excite some comment on the present problems of the female.

In short, I have done everything I could to prepare myself to interpret the female problem from *her* angle, as well as from my own, for the benefit of the casual male reader who would not be caught dead in such research. I hope to bring him up to date on this pending crisis which is hovering over us along with so many lesser problems like getting along with Russia, integration, and the relative values of various cigarette filters.

At times I have been most discouraged, believing like George Meredith that "Women will probably be the last animal civilized by man." That long-forgotten statement still holds good.

It is not easy for a man who has spent all his productive years as a physician to write an analytical essay about the female sex. He knows down deep in his heart that without women's good will and patronage he would have been hard put to meet his fundamental obligations to his family, the bill collectors, and society in general. His professional life, without the entertaining and enlightening antics peculiar to the sex, would have been a dreary chore. The female patient is a constant source of challenge, amusement and financial gain. Just why should *not* the medical profession appreciate her "in all her infinite variety?"

Male patients are a bore. Either they have some well-known disease or they haven't; or they are worried sick for fear of losing their true maleness—the power to reproduce. In searching for a reason for man's fluctuating blood pressure we consult the Dow-Jones averages rather than our text books, and if we inform him that his reproductive organs are functioning normally he goes home happy and we don't see him again for a year or more.

His wife, on the other hand, presents more perplexing problems than ever faced the United Nations. Her apparent illness may stem from a cheating or stingy husband, some other woman's mink coat, the disappointment over a new color rinse that didn't do all she expected for her hair, or any one of a thousand things that bear no relationship whatever to the supposed ailment with which she is at the moment engrossed. All this adds a spice and uncertainty which lights up the drab day a doctor endures treating truly sick people.

No man knows the workings of a woman's mind, but a doctor gets paid for guessing while such activities cause other men anguish and considerable financial loss. Freud said that after thirty years of research on the subject that he still had no idea as to what women wanted from life.

We doctors know that as a sex they are not angels, though as a rule they are a cut better than their male associates. They have most of the same problems that confuse the male, plus a multitude of new ones which have arisen as a result of man's abandonment of the famous dictum of Dr. Hertzler: "To keep them happy, keep them barefoot and pregnant."

Giving women shoes and contraceptives has also given them

time to think, and thinking women, like Shakespeare's Cassius, are dangerous because they think too much.

In addition to shoes and contraceptives we have given women gadgets galore to lighten their work load, and transportation and telephones so that they may communicate more readily with each other. All of this has added extra time for thinking, and as a result the modern woman is in a state of constant funk and frustration about her economic, emotional, romantic and social status.

Female researchers and psychologists have informed the ladies that they are only a "second sex," and as such must eternally suppress their normal personalities and pretend an inferiority toward the male in order that they may attract him. Eve knew all that, and so did the Nod maidens that married Cain and Seth, but they did not know that they were therefore supposed to be suffering from inferiority complexes.

Phyllis McGinley, writing in a woman's magazine recently, hit the nail squarely on the head when she stated that women are not superior to men, neither are they inferior; *they simply belong to a different race.* Though she did not so state, she implied that the only thing common between the sexes was the food they ate. I longed to say this, but did not dare to do so. Now I can hide behind the skirts of a woman in most of the critical remarks regarding her sisters that may appear in the text.

I hope to prove, by somewhat misquoting the Good Book, that woman's inheritance is indeed entirely different from our own. She is a lineal descendant of the females of the Land of Nod, and a repository for all the savage instincts of that alien tribe.

It is understood, I hope, that in the following pages I am not referring to my wife or yours, but simply trying to call your attention to the direction in which the wind is blowing. If I am forced to accuse women of harboring many characteristics which are contrary to the old image of a guiding light, I still must admit that I stand in reverence at the success many women have made of their associations with our sex.

Woman is indeed a half-civilized animal like the elephant,

willing to carry more than half the load but like that most
useful animal is liable to go berserk and wreck the whole
circus for no apparent reason. She is, nevertheless, the most
satisfying companion for man's travels through life. Like a
violin, she is equipped with only four strings ranging from
the high, sweet tones of an angel to the deep-throated growls
of the devil. If you play upon the instrument skillfully the
tones blend into the sweetest melody, but if you do not use
the bow properly a most discordant racket assails the ear
drums. Like fiddles, each woman has to be played somewhat
differently to bring out the best of her tones. Even a Strada-
varius will sound like a ten cent store instrument if not properly handled, and I've heard the most saintly of women sound
like common fish wives when rubbed the wrong way.

Women's magazines to the contrary, there are no competent
teachers in this most difficult of arts of making a woman's
strings quiver in melodious tune. I can only tell you what I
know about the instrument and hope that this will help you
to draw sweet harmony from it, even at the risk of a Roman
conflagration.

Life with Women

and

How to Survive it

1

I Give You Woman and May God Have Mercy on Your Souls

A woman is a foreign land
Of which, though there he settle young
A man will ne'er quite understand
The customs, politics, and tongue.
COVENTRY PATMORE

THE YEAR WAS 1912, my Junior year in medical school, the place the delivery room amphitheater of a Midwest teaching hospital, the time two A.M. It is a most appropriate setting for a lecture upon the vagaries of the female sex; here, as in no other place, the atmosphere is saturated with femininity. Here is woman stripped of all artificiality, busily engaged in her primal function; here the Captain's lady and Judy O'Grady are sisters under the skin, and sisters too of the hairy, ape-like creature of pre-historic time squatting in the darkness of her cave giving birth to man's more distant grandpas.

An amphitheater much resembles a cave at this hour of the night. Only the pit is illuminated with strong spotlights shining upon the delivery table and the mother-to-be. The nurses, flitting in and out of the shadows, shrouded in white gowns, masks and headress, remind one of strangely costumed savages. The white gowned spectators seated above are distinguishable only by the light reflected from the pit, and to one looking up at them they resemble stalagmites in a poorly lighted underground cavern.

The delivery room is a most appropriate setting for a lecture on the vagaries of the female.

The woman undergoing actual birth for the first time, strapped firmly to the table with her heels higher than her head, most likely sees herself as a potential sacrifice to some heathen god, with her doctor and nurses as high priest and priestesses. The Good Book says she must bear children in sorrow, so we will let her suffer while we bring on the other actors.

Our class of medical students had been alerted at nine P.M.; there would be a difficult delivery sometime during the night with the probable demonstration of the application of forceps. The Chief of Obstetrics would be in charge and we had better be there when the roll was called.

When we arrived the patient, an unmarried girl from the

local Florence Crittenden home, was in the crying room (well named). We were expected to examine her, listen to the fetal heart beat, register our guesses as to the sex and position of the child in the abdomen, and the likely presentation of the head as it entered the birth canal.

Diagnosing a baby's position through the abdominal walls of a husky young woman is like playing a piano while wearing boxing gloves, so we took our places in the dimly lighted recesses of the amphitheater not much the wiser.

The Chief of Obstetrics arrived and informed us that he'd decided to let nature take its course as long as there seemed to be no damage to the mother or babe. We settled down for a trial by labor, before art was called upon to speed up the process.

Hours passed, and at one thirty the nurses decided it was time to call the boss and get on with the party. Forceps were not demonstrated, but soon a baby girl was delivered.

Having successfully completed the practical part of our lesson, the obstetrician handed the rest of the job over to an intern and came to the rail of the gallery with the squirming girl child in his hands to give us the philosophical part.

"You are wondering," he began, "just why I did not use forceps or some of the stimulating drugs to terminate this labor hours ago, and you are probably cataloging the old man as a fuddy-duddy. I could have enjoyed the hours spent here in my own bed, but I took this method of bringing to your attention the most important qualification of a good obstetrician: the ability to sit on his hands. You know as well as I do that the principal indication for the application of forceps is the near approach of office hours, and that the after-effects of stimulants are not always what we wish them to be. Patience is a hard lesson for the young to learn, but here you see the results of it: a perfect baby without a scratch or scar, and a tired but healthy mother who has had the least possible exposure to infection. That is what you promise to work for every time you accept a maternity case.

"You are dealing here with the most efficient animal ever turned out on the evolutionary assembly line; nature will com-

plete the process of birth in a satisfactory manner without your
interference in forty-nine cases out of fifty. You earn your fee
by knowing when assistance is needed and being able to furnish it.

"Now I direct your attention to the babe which I am holding
in my hands. Here is the real enigma which has caused mankind more joy and sorrow than any other. To a physician she is
an animated crystal ball; if you can read her message correctly
you will be successful physicians. If you are masculine enough
to instill confidence in her mind, you will never lack for
patients; if you are too masculine and awake the animal within
her you will never lack for trouble."

Here he handed the babe to a waiting nurse and continued.
"This is only another illegitimate baby girl, which fortunately
looks like none of you, so you can lay your fears at rest. But her
potential is unlimited.

"Twenty-five years ago, as an intern of this hospital, I delivered just such another girl baby. Yesterday's paper was full of
the havoc she has caused; she was shot and killed in a jealous
rage by a prominent member of our nation's business world.
Before the New York reporters get tired of this sad tale families
will be broken up and businesses will topple.

"What twenty-five years will do to this baby you have just
seen delivered, no one knows. But we do know that she is perfectly formed and as healthy as a bear. From accumulated experience we can foretell a lot about her personality, and as doctors we need this illusive key for a successful practice among
her sex.

"If I may paraphrase an old quotation, 'Sex to a man is a
thing apart, a woman's whole existence.' The odds are against
her ever being a great builder of works of art and utility, a
deep thinker or philosopher, an interpreter of religious truths,
or a scientist probing into the secrets of the universe. All her
actions for the next fifty years are governed by those two tiny
glands within her abdomen called ovaries, for therein lies the
future of the human race. So why should she bother with such
things as bridges, buildings, manufacturing, interpreting the

scriptures, making laws for the conduct of mankind, or the secrets of the stars?

"She will enjoy the products of man's inventive genius and inquiring mind, and respect the laws he has laid down for the conduct of the race (at least in principle), but she will feel no twinges of conscience should occasion arise when disregard of them seems to be for the benefit of herself and her young.

"Her regard for truth is admirable, but in no way a compulsive emotion, and when the occasion calls for it she will be the most accomplished and enthusiastic liar.

"Always look upon her, gentlemen, as a female animal who looks over the male sex with a most critical eye that she may choose the best possible sire for her offsprings' future inherited characteristics. She will jealously guard the welfare of her young and search for a safe place in which to raise her brood.

"She will never be satisfied with anything, always seeking new experiences even in such fundamentals as food, clothing and the furnishings of her nest.

"She can think much faster than men on subjects related to the emotions, and she can out-talk or out-argue him on any subject simply by retiring into her female fortress and dismissing his arguments as silly and childlike.

"She resents man's position in the world and will worry herself sick trying to put him in what she considers to be his rightful place; if she succeeds, her scorn for the poor weakling will be awful to behold.

"She despises all other women and their offspring, but once an unfortunate child becomes motherless she is ready to add him to her brood and treat him as her own.

"She can repair anything so long as it can be done with a hairpin or a manicure set; give her a whole mechanic's tool chest and she cannot thread a nut upon a bolt.

"She has a quick and receptive brain and can compete with men on most any educational level, but everything she learns blots out some of her feminine instinct, and it seems that her accomplishments in the field of education reduce her capacity to function as a woman. Therefore the most learned women are often the poorest mothers. Her reasoning powers are purely a handicap in any crisis and are quickly discarded so her intuition may take over.

"She can be the kindest or the most cruel animal on earth (unless it be a cat playing with a mouse), and nobody, not even she herself, knows which mood will govern her tomorrow.

"She demands, and gets, the most luxurious surroundings her husband can afford, and can thrive on hardships which would kill *him* in a week.

"At some stages of her life she can be the most beautiful thing in nature, and at others the most grotesque shape in the animal kingdom.

"Above all she has the greatest instinct for survival of any animal and this reaction to assaults upon her physical being is the saving grace of all surgeons in keeping their mortality rates within limits. She is largely insensible to pain, and, more astonishing, seems to enjoy the sensation; consequently she will agree to any surgical procedure—and enjoy it.

Gentlemen, I give you woman.

"The riddle of the sphinx is elementary compared with her possible actions and reactions, but she was given to us by the Almighty with, I am sure, a major assist from the devil. We love her, cherish her, and often would like to choke her; but without her we doctors and the human race in general would be in one hell of a fix. Gentlemen, I give you Woman in all her infinite variety, and may God have mercy on your souls."

2

Dr. Peck's Do-It-Yourself Genesis

THE OLD DOCTOR tried to answer the question, "What is woman?" An earlier version of that same problem, "What are little girls made of?" begins to bother a boy at the age of four, and the answer continues to elude him for the rest of his natural life.

Between the ages of sixteen and twenty-five he may subscribe to the sugar and spice answer, or even to that of father Adam's rib as recorded in the second chapter of Genesis. But by the time he is thirty years of age, though he may still believe that she is "bone of his bone and flesh of his flesh," he has begun to wonder just what kind of brains the Good Lord stuffed her cranium with in the first place.

Anatomists tell us that there is no structural difference between the brains of the two sexes, but it would be hard to find a husband who wasn't convinced that his wife's brain was made of different stuff than his and had been installed

8

upside down or crossways. There must be some mixup in the wiring because the answer to any problem, trifling though it may be, always comes out differently when presented to the two sexes. Yet we are taught that both man and woman are chips from the same old block of wood.

I have pondered this problem for years and find the best explanation contained in that same First Book of Moses, third chapter. If read as a simple statement of man's origin, this account definitely shows woman to be of some strange root-stock found dwelling in the land of Nod on the east side of Eden, and other faraway places. (I do not mean Mother Eve, she was definitely the mother of the masculine portion of the human race, but no place in the Good Book is she credited with any daughters.)

Perhaps the reader will dismiss my comments by remarking that the story of man's creation is only a pretty allegory, or accuse me of being sacrilegious for trying to interpret the scriptures according to my own purpose. To the first, may I call attention to the fact that in the first chapter of Genesis the formation of the earth and the origin of life in the sea nicely conform to modern teaching upon these subjects. Why then must we dismiss the account of man's origins with a shrug? If Moses knew all of the important facts about the formation of the universe, how come he could wander off into fantasy in the very next chapter? For those who believe me scoffing at the Word, let us review the events chronicled in the book of Genesis and record them in the simple language of today.

In the beginning we find Father Adam tending the garden and running a zoo on the side. He also had to think up names for all of the animals and that was no small job without a crossword dictionary. Just consider the mental anguish he must have suffered giving birth to the name *gnu*. Being a man, he naturally bellyached about the job to the Big Boss. Parkinson's law was functioning then, even as it does today, and he could not feel happy and content without a couple of assistant managers, four subforemen, and most of all a cook. The Lord caused all of the animals to be paraded before Adam, but none of them seemed to fill the specifications he had in mind; no young executive wants a hairy ape for a stenographer or a bear for a junior-exec. Like his remote descendants, he complained that everything gave him a pain in the neck. Finally the Boss Man got fed up, gave him an anesthetic and removed a cervical rib; from it a helpmeet was constructed who filled the job most satisfactorily for the time being.

Adam, being an only child, was probably a tough nut to cope with and Eve doubtless had a pretty hectic time trying to please him, until she met the serpent over by the apple tree. This varmint advised her to use her sex to bring the old man off his high horse, and it worked wonderfully well. It got them both dispossessed, but who cares.

The serpent's advice worked wonderfully well.

The inevitable results soon appeared and were called Cain and Abel. Now that Eve discovered the cause of all this anguish, she postponed the multiplication and replenishment of the earth for awhile, but like most women she got careless in her old age and Seth appeared.

In the meantime Cain had become a farmer and Abel went to sheep herding. The Big Boss looked with favor on Abel's mutton, but turned a fishy eye on Cain's pumpkins. Being a true farmer, Cain felt that everybody was trying to short change him, and this insult made him so sore he bashed in Abel's skull and went over the hill, probably hunting a spot where pumpkins were classed as surplus and the parity price was satisfactory.

In his search for the Utopia where they pay you for not raising pumpkins, Cain wandered over into the land of Nod and there discovered some sort of female creature who could take his sperm and, by some lucky biological accident, made something of it. So Enoch was born. Seth came along later and consummated the same sort of union; he begat Enos and the human race was definitely in business.

Eve was a grandmother by this time, but unfortunately on the father's side, and any five year old with two grandmothers will tell you that is the wrong side. It is not surprising that she drops from sight never to be heard of again; we may assume that female troubles and age had caught up with her.

Adam, being a man with no such time limit on his virility, must also have married some of these Nod females. We are told that when he was three or four hundred years old he sired many sons and daughters, female parent or parents unknown.

Moses, the recorder of all these doings, was a gentleman; not wanting to stir up any controversy with his women folks, he left it up to the reader's imagination as to just what sort of a monkey, magpie or ringtailed cat these females from Nod called Papa and Mama.

Every man is entitled to his own opinion of the origin of the female sex, and following are my own conclusions. Adam was made of the dust from the ground, but the chronicler neglects to say how long it took to develop him. He was the last apple on the family tree and in no way resembled his distant ancestors. I am inclined to believe that the original rootstock was the wolf, or his milder cousin the dog. Man's habits and social behavior more closely resemble the canine than any other member of the zoo.

Being so different from the parent stock, Adam might have been destined to live and die an old bachelor. There was nothing living at that time that could mate with him, so his creator gave him a helpmeet constructed from spare parts of his own body.

Eve was not a true woman because she was constructed entirely from masculine materials. It is not likely that she would ever have been able to bear a daughter, as her basic ingredients were purely masculine. Cain, Abel and Seth received a double dose of male sex hormones and were the result of what stockmen call "line breeding," which fixes the inherited characteristics so firmly in the genes that they are dominant after many crosses with other stock. Down through the ages the man child has retained this maleness, regardless of his wife's efforts to change him.

This was a time of tumult and confusion in the development of life on this planet, and science tells us that most anything could happen and probably did. We are justified in believing that the girls over in Nod were also the end results of some of nature's experiments, experiments which probably began with lions and tigers. They were on hand when Cain arrived, and were probably the basis of the myth about the Amazons. The early Greeks believed that Hercules and Achilles overcame this tribe of superwomen, but I think Cain deserves the credit, and it is obvious from the results that he didn't use a bow and arrow to accomplish the feat. These ladies were also endowed with fixed personalities—the sum total of the traits of their feline ancestors—so here again we find the pattern pretty well fixed.

For those who would dismiss my reasoning as nonsense, I hope that they will stop right here and write a book of their own explaining why men are canine in their social natures, and why women more closely resemble the feline. I am willing to acknowledge that the traditional cat and dog role is some-what sublimated, in the male at least, during the period of courtship. But observe the husband and wife after the honeymoon period. The yowls and growls issuing from their dwelling remind the hearer of the battle between the Gingham Dog and the Calico Cat. Women have been compared to cats ever since men could use words, and for the best of reasons; they act like them. The cat is probably the smartest animal on earth, when it comes to the welfare and comfort of said cat.

The offspring of these unions of the Eden boys and the Nod girls were of course hybrids, products of the male or canine strain, and a female line which was highly flavored with the feline. Hybrids are usually stronger and more vigorous than the parent plants, and while those crossed by man are not fertile, Nature could have remedied this deficiency and apparently did. These hybrids were also problem children, inheriting the murderous disposition of Cain and the catlike guile of their mothers. Their brains were more developed and their propensity for getting into trouble more marked.

Within a few generations the Lord decided to drown them all, but in a moment of weakness He saved Noah and his family (the best of a bad lot) so as not to have to start from scratch again. Noah was a good man, but the genes were still there and in a few short generations we find his offspring once again trying to exterminate each other; a trait that seems to be the dominant one even to this day.

To the unthinking and the prejudiced, the following pages may sound a bit cattified, but it is not intentional and merely the result of my long association with the female sex. I would not intentionally make a disparaging remark about women because I love them all. And I should; women paid the rent for my office, educated my children and kept my table bountifully supplied with the good things of life. Without them I and most other physicians would be on relief. But they are strangers to every man, and all I can hope to do is to explain some of their thought processes to my fellow man so that he may at least understand what hit him.

So gather round, boys. We will catch one of those soft little pussycats that has made man's life so complicated and so satisfying and place her under a microscope. We will apply some scientific method and much speculation to find out what makes her act the way she does.

3

Darling Daughters of Satan

There was a little girl
Who had a little curl
Right in the middle of her forehead;
And when she was good
She was very, very good
But when she was bad she was horrid.
HENRY WADSWORTH LONGFELLOW

I₉ THIS ESSAY is to progress in an orderly manner, the next task should be an analysis of the child and adolescent girl, her mental and physical progress. As far as I know this has never been successfully done and I am not nut enough to expect to accomplish it here. I feel myself well qualified for the task, however. I never had any girl playmates during my formative years, nor any daughters to study in my more mature age, and the less one knows about his subject and the farther away he is from it, the more authoritatively he can discuss it.

Since the conception of this work, I have racked my brains and the public libraries without success for a study of the girl child that could in any way compare with *Huck Finn* or Tarkington's *Penrod*. Mark Twain's Susie was a beautiful character, and if she measured up to her daddy's opinion of her, it is well that she passed from this earth before she had run up against the realities of life. I do not believe any man is truly qualified to search the brain of the adolescent female, and certainly no woman would be so treacherous to her sex as to attempt it.

My only point of observation of the growing female has been that of a family doctor. In the course of thirty years' practice I have met some little angels and some little devils and usually the more angelic they looked the more likely they were to be daughters of Satan himself. For some unaccountable reason this quirk seems to carry on into adult life; the beautiful female is conscious of her power to make jackasses of the male sex and continues to use it as long as she can. Fortunately she usually loses her allure much earlier than her sisters not so gifted in appearance.

By the time she is three years old, she is preparing herself
for motherhood.

The first difference between the female child and her male counterpart seems to be the desperate hurry she's in to arrive at a fruitful stage, compared to the diffident manner in which the boy approaches puberty. By the time she is three years old, the girl child is preparing herself for motherhood with dolls, playing house, and eavesdropping on the cat having kittens.

All the while her brother's interests are as far from domesticity as possible. He skates all over the pond, evading the thin ice by inches time and again, and when finally he does fall in it is probably because some girl shoved him; but as soon as *she* buckles on her skates she makes a bee-line for the treacherous hole and jumps in headlong as though there were a box of candy at the bottom of it.

Many a time during home deliveries I have looked up and found the little girls of the family peeking around the bedroom door. Investigation found their brothers hiding under beds, stiff with fear that the stork might grab them and carry them off to some less happy home, just as their dads had threatened if they were naughty. As the child goes, so does the adult; any woman would break her neck in order to attend another's delivery, but a man wouldn't get within a mile of the scene without being dragged by a wailing wife and morbid conventions.

As the old doctor said, the female admires truthfulness in others but seldom feels any compulsion to practice the art; even as a child she will dream up impossible stories to save herself from punishment. You can usually tell when a boy is manhandling the truth by his hang-dog expression, but little angel-face will gaze up at you with those big soulful eyes and spin off ten big black lies faster than most males could think up one.

Following are two illustrations showing the female reaction, one in a child of six, and the other in a young lady of fourteen when romance begins to color the thoughts.

One hot summer afternoon I was called to a neighboring town on an emergency; the mother who telephoned was too excited to tell me the details. Upon arrival, I learned that two little girls of five or six years of age had been playing in the then ever present outhouse, and a little brother, age three, had joined them. Soon the girls ran screaming to their mother with the news that Johnnie had fallen through the hole into the pit beneath. Fortunately father was at home and he rushed out, overturned the building, jumped into the hole and rescued the boy. When I arrived father and son were lying on the lawn with mother spraying the hose on them. The boy had lit upon a broken lamp chimney and had quite a scalp wound on the head, but seemed generally no worse for his adventure. While I was dressing his wound I noticed that he showed a lot of hostility toward his sister, who was trying to appear quite solicitous but nevertheless remaining in the background.

It all looked fishy to me; although the victim could only say "bad sister" I decided to investigate. When his soiled clothing was removed I noticed a friction burn on his shoulder; I got a wire, fitted it into the circumference of the hole in the seat, and then tried to pass it down over the child's shoulders. That boy didn't fall—he had been pushed, and pushed *hard*. When faced with this accusation the little girl promptly and sweetly blamed it on her friend who had discreetly made for home as soon as the ruckus started.

Her father believed her; nobody that looked so truthful and saintlike could think of doing such a thing in the first place, and certainly was incapable of lying about it afterwards. But her mother remembered how little girls hate to have little brothers tag along and she whaled the daylights out of that young lady. I naturally delayed my departure to enjoy the spectacle.

The other episode involved a pretty fourteen year old who arrived home at midnight, long after the hour she had been told to return. She tearfully informed her parents that she had been raped. Of course the father went slightly crazy, but his anxiety for his child overcame his murderous instincts and he brought the ravished maiden to my home. Examination showed no bruises, torn garments or evidence of a struggle; she had definitely not suffered from any crime upon her person.

Pretending that I had to make a report for the officers of the law, I quizzed the young lady carefully. It seemed that while coming home from the picture show a certain boy had overpowered her and dragged her to the ball park, where the deed was supposed to have taken place. Her father had failed to ask her who the assailant was, and when I got to that question she hesitated. I told her she would be arrested herself if she did not answer. She thought for a minute, but a minute was not long enough, and she made her mistake.

"It was Bobby Jones." This was greeted with hoots of laughter from me and some choice swearing from her dad.

"Why, you little liar," he said. "Bobby Jones isn't big enough to take a lollipop away from you! You come clean with the truth or I'll spank you good right here."

"If I do, will you promise not to whip me?" she tried to bargain.

"I don't know, but I'll sure beat the tar out of you if you don't," he replied.

So we got an approximation of the true story. She and a girl friend had stayed through the picture show twice, and when they parted at the corner they decided to spring the rape story on their parents to avoid a licking for being so late. The other girl was lucky; her parents slept soundly and did not awaken when she slipped into the house. It was fortunate for everybody that the girls did not rehearse their story beforehand, as a little thought would have made them pick a more likely victim than poor little Bobby Jones.

Of course both these stories of scheming females are extreme, but for that reason I remember them in detail. Men have gone to jail on just such silly evidence, and little brothers have probably suffered even worse fates from older sisters' revenge.

The point I wish to make is that, even as a child, the female is inclined to color any story to her own advantage regardless of its consequences.

Every doctor learns to take the history as the female gives it, and then draws upon his experience with the sex and the circumstances to arrive at his own conclusions. I have often wondered how judges and attorneys handle these matters, particularly in regard to sex crimes. When I hear a tale about such matters and the female did not show signs of a battle, I am always reminded of the old lady and the tramp. She informed him that he could not have his way with her unless he tied her up, and that there was a rope hanging behind the kitchen door.

Rearranging the circumstances is not a crime to the female, it is simply a way of getting along with the ethical demands of a society fashioned and enforced by the stronger and more bull-headed males. Whether girls are born with this attribute, I do not know, but their mothers begin educating them pretty soon thereafter.

Regardless of what little hellions they may be, they soon assume the demeanor of an angel and are dressed to confirm the illusion. They seem so dainty and timid, and yet some of them will grab a kitten by the neck and drown it in the wash bowl without a twinge of conscience. They will put up with hypos, stitches and other repair operations without a sound, while their brothers have to have an anesthetic to remove a tiny splinter from a thumb.

The girls will put up with hypos while their brothers suffer the tortures of the damned.

When I was practicing medicine I always tried to postpone the removal of tonsils as long as possible, but if it became necessary I liked to do the operation under local anesthetic. I found that I could operate on my girl patients easily by the time they were twelve years of age; they would sit up with their mouths open like hungry baby robins and actually seemed to get a great kick out of the procedure. The boys, however, would suffer the tortures of the damned until they were at least seventeen or eighteen.

This quality carries on through adulthood. I have never seen a woman faint at the sight of a bloody mess unless there was some man handy to catch her, while men will often faint at the sight of a hypodermic. In the small towns of an earlier day, when automobile wrecks were not so commonplace, everybody on the street would follow the ambulance to the doctor's office. I made a rule that all the men should go outdoors before they fainted and that all the females handy should put on gowns and get busy helping me clean up the mess. The female is much more durable than the male in gory situations.

One night I was called to a desert ranchhouse some thirty miles from my office and found a woman bleeding badly from a miscarriage. Things had to be done in a hurry, so I pulled her over to the side of the bed and instructed the husband to support her knees while I worked. After about two minutes, I noticed the man getting white around the ears and breathing heavily. Shock treatment was in order; I told him that if he fainted now he might lose his wife. He hung on until I was about through and then gasped, "Doc, can I faint now?" His wife snapped, "Yes, you big baby, go ahead and faint." He promptly did, and as he fell he cut his head on the base of the stove and it took several stitches to repair the damage. I put in the stitches without any anesthetic whatever; he was too far gone to notice the pain. He was six feet tall and weighed two hundred pounds, so I let him lie there until he was able to get up himself. Females are manufactured out of rawhide and the sturdiest oak, and are a constant source of surprise and delight to the physician who ministers to them.

In the previous chapter, the origin of the human species as recorded by Moses was somewhat expanded. Should Moses be around to read it, he might share the bewilderment of most authors when the proofs come back from the editorial rooms of the publishing firm. However, we proved the truth of Miss McGinley's assertion that women were of a different race and could not be expected to share all of man's thoughts and ambitions. The old obstetrician in Chapter One listed a few of those deviations from the normal, and the task now is to explain the reasons for such vagaries.

There is little difference to be noted in the first few years of life between the male child and his sister; he is perhaps larger boned and slower in his development, but at the early ages both sexes fight like little wild cats and (when the notion strikes them) play like kittens. However, about the fourth year the female child discovers that her masculine playmate has an external decoration which was denied her, and trouble begins. She sees that this appendage is not only a handy thing to take on a picnic, but is also a built-in fixture for the amusement of its possessor. She feels cheated by nature, and thus a resentment is started toward the opposite sex which continues until old age, when the shoe is on the other foot. (Then Grandma knits and smiles when Grandpa walks the floor in misery because his plumbing facilities are not behaving as they should. She neither feels nor demonstrates any sympathy, believing that it serves the old goat right for trying to wear the thing out when he was younger.)

About the fourth year a resentment is started toward the opposite sex which continues until old age.

The little girl, for all of her built-in wisdom, cannot look ahead to this time of fulfillment and revenge. So her envy grows with each passing year, and envy in a female is an all-engrossing passion. The researchers tell us that about this time she acquires an inferiority complex in relations with the male, and forever after is obsessed with the idea of making him suffer for his favored anatomy. She tries with all her might to reduce him to the status of a satellite moon, orbiting about herself. Keep this in mind; it will explain a lot about her actions in later years.

She also discovers that the boy is favored in other ways: he is allowed to get as dirty as he wishes, to wear simpler clothes, and is never commanded to act like a lady. An even more disturbing fact seems to be that, because of his special appendage or in spite of it, he seems to be growing stronger. He can now best her in personal combat. So, like all women before her, she turns to subterfuge to gain her lost mastery of the situation; her estimation of her own importance and ego is based upon the amount of guile she can display in achieving her desires.

If your darling daughter shows too much proficiency in sports of a masculine nature, you are cursed by that old jingle about whistling girls and crowing hens never coming to very good ends. So you direct her attention to dolls and play houses, and she learns by watching mommy that her role requires her to play her part to the hilt.

All of this may sound as though I did not hold a very high opinion of my little girl patients, but nothing could be further from the truth; I loved every little angel and devil among them. They seemed to return my affection and never held a grudge when I found it necessary to expose their perfidy. When brought to see the doctor, they flew onto my lap like a bird to its nest, and if I had to hurt them a bit during an examination they were brave little soldiers. As they grew up and began to have boy troubles they slipped in without their mothers and squalled their eyes out upon my more or less sympathetic shoulder. But no man who has ever held a little feminine bundle of love and affection to his breast and been called papa or grandpa by those delightful lisping lips will, for one moment, believe that this creature would be capable of such perfidy or such bravery as I have described. And I do not blame him; I feel the same way myself. However, we males must realize that she, like Minerva, was born a fully developed female. From the cradle she is aware of the difficult role she must play and she has to play it by ear. Today an angel, tomorrow a calculating little devil, the day after a heroine. You would, in your manly ignorance, shield her from the cruel and mercenary world and keep her an innocent child forever; unfortunately she has a mission in life and will have no part of your sheltering dreams.

Just remember that while you are holding her in your protecting arms and unconsciously praying that she will never have to grow up and face the stern realities, she is way ahead of you, dreaming of the time when she can wear lipstick and high heeled shoes. And if it is any comfort, let me assure you that the time will come when some *other* man will echo your sentiments about her and pray: "Backward, turn backward, O time in your flight, and make her a child again, just for tonight . . . so I can spank the daylights out of her without getting a call from her attorney tomorrow."

4

Magnificent Enigma—
the Adolescent Female

There goes a vague mind in a vogue body.
ANONYMOUS

THE URGENT SPEED with which a female child proceeds toward her destiny of mature womanhood becomes frantic haste between the ages of twelve and fifteen. No butterfly ever struggled harder to emerge from his cocoon and spread his silky wings upon the morning air than does the feminine adolescent in trying to convince her mother that she is now old enough for mascara and black nylon stockings.

Last week, when she smiled, her mouth looked like a badly used bedspring, with wires running this way and that from tooth to tooth; today her smile resembles a white-centered petunia with red borders. Suddenly her breasts pop out, and if they don't she pops them out herself by stuffing old stockings in her mother's brassiere and wearing that. Yesterday her legs were purely functional members, stretching from her body to the ground; today they show the promise that has turned men's heads and paralyzed their brains, literally ever since Eve.

But the surface change is of minor importance. It is the rush with which her internal organs prepare themselves for a possible pregnancy that is astounding. Today she is a little girl; tomorrow she is suffering from what women call "the curse" and undergoing all the mental fireworks and body tensions that accompany that manifestation of fertility.

At her menstrual times she may seem to be mad all the time. There is reason for that: Nature prepares her for this ordeal by storing an excess of fluid in her tissues and she feels like a stuffed toad for a few days before the onset of each period. Some women suffer a man-sized bellyache, and it behooves you to act sympathetic if you do not want your eyes scratched out.

Now her instruction in evading the truth begins to pay off; she is in the big leagues where woman's every action and statement is meant to camouflage and evade the real issues and to attract the male's attention to her female loveliness and desirability. And the things she has to endure to perfect herself in this deceptive art would drive her masculine counterpart to the funny house in short order. The only analogy that man's brain could understand would be for a man to disguise himself as a worm, put himself on a hook and try, by his squirming, to attract the biggest trout in the pool; once the fish grabs the bait, sock the hook into his own jaw and then escape onto the bank and try valiantly to land himself. Show me the *man* who can play the role of bait and fisherman at the same time.

There are a lot of taboos that govern the actions of this worm: she must always look cool and unperturbed, inviting and yet repelling advances.

She must never be caught sweating; a few tiny pearls of perspiration upon her brow may be gently tapped with her hankie, but to break out in such an animal reaction as a good old sweat and to enjoy the pleasure of wiping one's face with a shirt sleeve or a big bandana handkerchief is forever denied her; besides, it would wreck her mascara and cause her face to look like a melting strawberry ice cream cone.

She must never expectorate when in the presence of the opposite sex, nor sit with her heels more than two inches off the floor.

She must not relieve the wind in the willows by a good

honest belch, or by the method described by Mark Twain in *1601.*

No matter how she may itch she must never scratch, or, if the irritated spot should be out of reach, rub her back against a door jamb like a pig on a post, as is the privilege of her boy friend.

If she would wear barefoot sandals and no stockings, she must also expose some of the thighs in hopes the male's attention will not wander to her poor misshapen feet. Of course the girl whose thighs look like pillows should always leave her shape to the imagination of the beholder.

No matter how generously nature and candy counters have endowed her, she must never have an abdomen which protrudes beyond a line running from her shin to her ankles.

She must smell at all times "Mighty like a Rose" instead of like a sweaty horse.

She must consume food like a humming bird on a trumpet vine, and never pick her teeth.

She must never, under any circumstances, show the least sign of intelligence and must be forever ready to admire and agree to every silly observation uttered by a male.

She must keep the fires within her under control so that they impart a glow to her personality, and have enough fluid in her fire extinguisher to quell the gleam in her escort's eye so a holocaust can be avoided until she is prepared to cope with it.

Not all women become perfect in these difficult arts. Consequently there are a lot of old maids and strong-minded business women running around loose, hating themselves and pestering their medical advisers with their frustrations.

But once a worm-woman has the fish-man on the hook, her natural moods become most unpredictable. Today she wants to be treated like a white kitten with a pink bow around its neck, tomorrow she wants her man to knock her about a bit, and the third day she despises the whole masculine portion of humanity.

Sometimes the girls bring these problems to their physician friend, and Solomon himself would be stumped for an answer.

I remember one little white kitten who came into my office, her face the picture of woe. After she had had her bawl on the old man's shoulder, she told the following story: She was engaged to a nice boy, and as they walked home the night before she felt like being roughed-up a bit, so she informed him that she did not intend to allow him to kiss her good-night.

Instead of grabbing her and using cave man tactics to subdue this revolt, he meekly answered, "All right, Nellie, if you do not desire that show of affection at this time, I will refrain." She was fit to be tied! She swore that she would never speak to him again, and as for loving and respecting him—it was impossible. She even cast doubts on his masculinity.

There was nothing I could say to comfort her, but I made it a point to talk with the boy, casually mentioning that sometimes girls prefer a cave man to a modern gentleman. The next time I saw his fiancée she bore the traces of a beautiful shiner peeping through her make-up and was radiantly happy.

Remember that the old doctor told us to regard woman as a peculiarly adroit and competent animal. At the age of fourteen or fifteen she is interested in all men and searching for that individual who will impart genes which, coupled with her own, will make for more handsome and competent little animals. This is not the girl you see nor the girl she would have you know; it is the Nod woman who is buried deep within her.

That woman, like all savage animals, is subject to periods of apparent insanity. Do not be surprised if the sex urge overcomes natural sagacity and she marries a wild and worthless mate who appeals only to her animal nature. It was Sam Levenson, I believe, who said the father of a female child of fifteen to twenty should not be too surprised if his daughter comes home some night and announces that she has married a bear.

This is the period over which poets and novelists rave, and it is probably the only time in her existence when a woman marries for love and nothing else. (Love meaning, of course, that infernal whip which nature uses to drive her helpless victims headlong toward their destiny of multiplying and replenishing the earth.)

Now that we have this young lady all rigged out in her

deceptions and camouflage, ready for the Hymeneal rites, I feel
that it is my duty to discuss what Margaret Mead calls the
post-Korean mating plan.

It seems that mothers are most responsible for this phenome-
non, and so, being a man, I am against it. And all through life
I think you will find that most things that women advocate are
wrong in principle and will lead to no good end if they are
carried out. Take this idea of mixing up the sexes in parties
and games when they are still natural adversaries and not yet
softened toward each other by the development of sex
emotions.

Children are encouraged to pair off at this tender age and
no girl child is considered a success unless she is going steady
by the time she is fourteen years old. Naturally she finds her
steady partner within her own age group and there the trouble
starts; she is at least two years older in development than the
boy and so is most likely to begin calling the tunes and leading
him before he becomes aware of what it is all about, and she
continues to do so from that day onward. These babies are
supposed to cleave to each other forsaking all others.

When they reach the mature age of eighteen or so they
naturally get married, and if the respective fathers and mothers
are able to support them, begin to multiply and replenish the
earth. They go about this chore with great enthusiasm. According to the above mentioned anthropologist, these fathers just
love to care for tiny babies. If this last conclusion of hers is a
true picture of the situation, I am happy that I am an old man
and nearing the point when I will no longer be interested in
the human race nor things that happen upon this mundane
sphere.

In my time I have seen caponized roosters that cheerfully
took over the mothering of a brood of incubator chicks, but
never did I see an animal that bore testicles engaged in such a
feminine pastime. It is true that the male bass hovers over the
eggs until they hatch, but once the small fry are big enough
to swim he eats as many as he can catch, so we cannot attribute
his nesting actions to purely domestic responsibility. The natural human male reaction to offspring is a mixture of the canine

plus a bit of the feline which he has inherited through his mother's blood. He either ignores his offspring as does the dog or has to stifle a tom-cat desire to destroy them, believing such action is an aid to romance.

A man who is only interested in little babies may not be stirred by his inherited tendency to wander from flower to flower seeking the sweetest, but I have my doubts. Even though he may be married to his steady of five years, still on some enchanted evening, across a crowded room he may see a stranger that will make his little hen look as if she were moulting. Will his love for babies conquer his wanderlust? I doubt it, and statistics bear me out. We know that divorce is three times as common in girls who marry around eighteen as among those that postpone the wedding day until they are twenty-three or four.

Perhaps the mother of all these lovely babies also looks around the room, and being more forthright in her training than was Maude Muller with her plaintive cry "It might have been," does something about it instead of dreaming. Whoever is at fault, it is those same babies that suffer. Once they get too old to need diaper service, papa loses interest in them and they grow up in broken homes, or else in homes in which the parents have no more love for each other, which is just as bad. If children are denied the safety of a home where the parents love and respect each other, parents are responsible before God for the little psychopaths they turn out upon society.

There is another serious drawback to this early dating and going steady: the unfortunate male is denied the society of his fellows. At this age a man's love for his gang is a much deeper and lasting emotion than any he can feel for the opposite sex. If a boy of eighteen or twenty were told that he was to be marooned on a desert island and could take along only one companion, four out of five true males would choose a buddy rather than a steady girl friend. Then the two of them could build a raft and try to make it to an island where there were some females.

Romantic love means just that: building your own raft and finding your own girl when you yourself are ready. There is no romance connected with a girl you have known intimately ever since you were fourteen. If the boy gets through college before he has to assume the responsibility of being a father and husband he makes lasting friendships with the fellows in his class and fraternity. His female friendships are strictly temporary unless some dame is more handy with her lasso than he is with his heels. If you break a colt and put him to work too soon, he never grows up to his potentialities and is always a browbeaten little runt of a pony that is good only for fox feed.

How can a boy who is worried about bills, his wife's contentment and the baby's measles concentrate on his studies and develop into the man he should be in later life? He only wants a few dependents on his draft classification card and once he has them he feels that he must punish himself by taking over their care. This post-Korean marriage pattern that is of so much interest to the anthropologists would likely go up in smoke if the Selective Service Act were repealed.

Every young girl should stop and think for a minute when her twenty year old boy friend takes the idea of quick marriage too seriously. Is he willing to take on the responsibilities of a family because he loves her so much that he cannot live without her another day and knows that their parents will pay the bills, or is he secretly planning to get her pregnant so that he can claim a hardship case when Uncle Sam calls him to duty? Have pity on the poor girl who fails to get into an interesting condition right away; she is likely to suffer the same fate as the wife of that Middle Eastern potentate and be cast off for somebody that is more fertile and makes haste to prove the fact. All this isn't such a strong foundation on which to build a happy marital union; the cement is likely to wash out of the cracks pretty fast and the whole structure may fall down once hubby is twenty-six years old. Then the little dependents are left to pay the bill in an unhappy life.

Stop a minute and consider the fact that this boy must live with himself a good many years after the two he spends in the Army. Do you want your daughter to serve as a brood mare just to keep some lily-livered male from having to serve his proper time for his country? Better that she remain a spinster with a job until she finds a man whose emotions toward her are not those of a farmer planning on increasing his herd.

If you would have your boy keep his self-respect, counsel him against these draft-dodging marriages. He was endowed with the necessary appendages which classify him as a male; see to it that he grows up with a full knowledge of a man's responsibilities and do all in your power to help him discharge them as a man should. Life is not going to be ruined by the loss of a couple of years in the service; in fact it may be made more worthwhile. He may gain the world, but if he loses his self-respect nothing else can replace it and he is a marked man in his own soul.

Man does not live for bread alone; neither does he live for the duties of a nursemaid and the joy connected with fixing formula and changing diapers. Both these things may be necessary, but let him be a boy and enjoy all of life's experiences at a time when his nature is ripe for the appreciation thereof.

You fathers of girl babies, marry them off as soon as you get the opportunity, if that is what you wish. But please protect your boy from such unnatural burdens until his back is strong enough to carry them. With all woman's newly acquired rights, the world is still run by men in the relationships between nations. Give your son an opportunity to grow into man's estate unencumbered by family duties until he has developed his personality by many experiences. He cannot become a man without them. Some of these teen-age marriages work out satisfactorily but the majority of them wind up on the rocks; nature to the contrary, neither the girl nor her mate is ready to settle down to the difficult business of raising children. And babies surely will arrive to muddy up the limpid waters of true love before affection and a feeling of partnership have had time to flower. There is nothing so tragic as a twenty year old mother trying to make a place in the world for herself and two or three little children, or a boy-father taking it on the lam because so much responsibility frightens him to distraction.

Now comes the time when mature men should draw their

somewhat soiled robes of chastity about them and avoid any situations wherein opportunities might arise for sex-crazy girls to imagine themselves desperately in love with them.

Now the woman's desire for security and a comfortable nest in which to raise her young takes over, and she is much more attracted to older men who are better established than to the boys who filled her thoughts at an earlier age. This change in her hunting habits is all very well for the children-to-be, but it is tough on the relief rolls, filling the country with elderly widows. (Even if the partners are of the same age, chances are that the woman will live five or ten years longer than her mate; when she marries an older man her period of widowhood is much increased.)

This arrangement is perfectly satisfactory with the younger men; they will never be able to understand how a woman can pant for some decrepit old goat of twenty-five who has a steady job, and pass up their own youthful charms. But owing to the fact that a youth has no overwhelming desire to take on the responsibilities of the marriage state, he is somewhat relieved when he is no longer the target of the lady's amorous glances and is free once again to play the field.

Lord Byron said (to put it exactly this time): "Man's love is of man's life a thing apart, 'tis woman's whole existence," and he might have added that courtship and marriage are also strictly her business and probably would never be accomplished if she did not take the initiative. I have talked to a lot of married men and never found one who was quite sure how he had come to be engaged or who would confess that he had thought seriously about the matter until it was an accomplished fact.

At this stage the father of such a girl is astonished at the behavior of his wife. She knows the temptations that beset her daughter's path and becomes feverishly intent upon getting the girl safely married. He naturally thinks his wife's patience has worn thin because of the raids upon her stocking supply and the messy bathrooms, but her worries have a deeper meaning. About all the old man can do is keep the shotgun loaded and hope for the best.

A girl in her teens regards her mother much as the adolescent son does his father. To the boy the old man is just one cut above a moron and slipping fast.

To the boy, the old man is just one cut above a moron and slipping fast.

It is a father's duty to realize that the pangs and fears of his own developing period were but a pallid thing compared to the storm raging within his daughter's breast. At this moment anything that wears pants is to her a near-god or a near-devil. Pop can be a real rock of refuge for his troubled daughter if he will make himself available.

If she gets into trouble, old dad too often pictures himself the wronged parent of the ancient meller-drammer, calls her all kinds of unmentionable things and drives her away.

She then slips into her doctor's office like a wounded animal and weeps out her story upon his already tear-stained shoulder.

Sometimes I was able to bring about a happy ending but more often all I could offer was sympathy and a few curses against man's inhumanity to man, or rather women.

I will always remember one case in which the girl asked me to meet her at my office long after office hours. She had been a star patient in her growing up years, so I complied. Same old story: the boy willing to marry her, but the father making threats to kill him and telling her never to darken his doorway again. I went into the record room and looked up the card of this particular family; those cards told the history of that town more fully than St. Peter's record book. One card showed Mary Jones: examined April about twenty years before; found to be pregnant. The next entry showed Mary Jones Smith: delivered of a daughter the next October. I called up the irate dad and

A family doctor's history cards have a way of hanging around long after juvenile antics are forgotten.

informed him that his daughter was in my consultation room; he began to spout. I let him boil and thunder for a few minutes and then remarked that I had been doing a bit of research among the old records and had found some interesting entries. Did he wish me to allow the girl to read them?

The old volcano suddenly changed to a pleading lamb. "Please, oh, please, Doc, burn that old card up, tell her to come on home—I've had a change of heart." I let the girl talk to her humble parent, and her joy was beautiful to see. She swore I was the most wonderful doctor in the world. I did not explain my method of working miracles, nor show her the evidence of her parents' coltish days. She had a nice wedding and it was easy for me to lie a little and insert "premature" upon the ensuing birth certificate.

You were young once too, Pop, and if you didn't get some girl into trouble it was not because of lack of effort. A family doctor's history cards have a way of hanging around long after your juvenile antics are forgotten. So be good to your "little girl." Someday you may be living in the same house with her again, and then the shoe will be on the other foot.

1159971

5

Crimes Committed in the Name of Beauty

IT IS TO be expected that any female who has read this far in this little book is likely to heave it into the trash can with the proper amount of fury and express her opinion of the author in fervent if inadequate blasphemy. Going on this assumption, we males can now relax and pick her to pieces at our leisure, without fear of interruption.

We have twisted the first book of Moses around to suit our purposes, and proved to masculine satisfaction that the female of the species is not of the species at all, but rather a termite kind of animal who has nibbled her way into our hearts and homes.

Too many books have been written about women, but I never have seen one in which the author was not directing the reader's thoughts, perhaps unconsciously, toward one specific individual. He either loved her and painted her with rose tinted brushes, or hated her and mixed fire and brimstone in his paintpots. He was prone to play upon only one string, emphasizing only one facet of her personality or appearance, particularly the effect she had upon those members of the male sex with whom she came in contact. All of those things are proper in their place, but in a book about women in general we should follow the scientific approach and begin our description by sketching the physical appearance of the creatures we are dissecting.

First we must reduce women to a common denominator, and view them in the natural state. Clothes do not make the woman, but they do serve as an excellent camouflage. To get at the truth of the matter, we must enforce the demands made upon the "stripper" and peel off the buttons and veils.

Beauty unadorned appeals strongly to the male's idea of the ludicrous (with the exception of those engaged in the practice of medicine, whose attentions are focused only upon the portion of anatomy which may contain pathological tissues). One nude female in the proper surroundings may be the most beautiful and desirable creature in the world; a random group of six seen in the buff by daylight looks a bit ridiculous.

We know that our boys were under great mental and physical strain during the action in the Pacific during World War II, and under such circumstances a man's sexual desires seem stronger than they ever are in civilian life. I suppose it is nature's way of insuring the perpetuation of the race; when a man feels that he may die tomorrow he has a compelling urge to breed today. But even then his sense of the grotesque sometimes overcomes his lust.

This tale was told me by a marine officer who was in charge of a detachment quartered upon one of the smaller islands of the South Pacific and illustrates this point. The brush was pretty heavy around their beach camp, so it was necessary for them to clear a path through the jungle that they might reach a clearing big enough for a drill field and target range. This path led them near a favorite swimming hole of the native ladies. Beauty was used to swimming unadorned in that region, and so the girls bathed in the buff. After a few days the local chief called upon the base commander and complained about the laughter of the soldiers as they passed by this maidens' bower. The American officer, anxious to retain the natives' good will and respect, offered to change the path or to erect a screen so the ladies would be shielded from masculine eyes during afternoon water sports. This did not suit the chief, and he explained, "No, our women like to have the boys look at them, but they do not like to have them laugh out loud at what they see." So another burden was added to the heavy load our soldiers had to bear, suppression of their natural instincts in still another way.

Had one of these soldiers met a solitary native girl in the moonlight, it would have been a safe bet that there would have been another story like the one about Bloody Mary's granddaughter and the lieutenant in *Tales of the South Pacific*.

Even in our supposedly more enlightened civilization, a young woman walking down the street in the briefest of shorts and the most skimpy halter tosses her head in satisfaction when someone whistles at her, but is likely to slap the guy who laughs. And believe it or not, laughter is the more common emotion stirring in the breast of the predatory male. Billie Burke, in her book *A Feather on My Nose*, says, "Women enjoy sex, but only man thinks it's funny."

Of course there are women, and men too, who would have made fine models for those old Greek marble chippers, but they are rare indeed. Women in the nude are more mirth-provoking because of the fact that men look about as bad when dressed as they do in the buff, while the corsetières have done a lot to bolster up the female form divine. Man should give thanks for these benefactors of the female sex. If the girls would stop there, much would be added to the pleasure of viewing the result. However they seem to think that if a little camouflage is good, a whole lot is better.

The crimes committed by women upon their hair, their faces and their garments, all of which are supposed to enhance the beauty of the view, shock the tender masculine nervous system. These crimes will be taken up in detail shortly, but first we must look at the motivation and psychology behind all this fashionable camouflage.

The early twenties is the time of fruition of all the training your lady friend has had from the time of infancy. The first and

The corsetieres have done a lot to bolster up the female form divine.

most important goal of her life is about to be achieved. She has gone through the battle with every other female hand raised against her (with the possible exception of her mother's) and has resisted the efforts of predatory males to reduce her to the status of a concubine.

At this age all women are beautiful and appealing to the opposite sex, with the possible exception of those who are overly endowed with fat. (There is a deep-seated belief that all young animals who are too well upholstered are deficient in their sexual development, and though their faces are the most beautiful of all, the boys are difficult to attract.)

This should be the happiest time in a woman's life, but unfortunately it is marred by anxiety and cutthroat competition for the most eligible males.

Poor girl, she is ordained like the apostles, to be a fisher of men, but before she ever wets a line she knows that the per-

centages are against her catching anything better than a mud-
cat. The armed forces discourage her right from the start with
their statistics regarding male fitness. They report that forty per
cent of the males examined are such poor physical specimens
that they are unfit to carry a gun or even to act as baby sitters
for the officers' families. Unfortunately for you, they neglect to
give the percentages of female rejectees for physical and mental reasons in the WACs. Since the female population is greater
than the male, it stands to reason that at least half of the girls
are doomed to spinsterhood, or at best to wind up with a poor
fish indeed. It is a gloomy prospect and probably the cause of
many of the mental aberrations and brain storms which afflict
women in later life.

These anxieties never affect the male and so are difficult for
you to understand; you were born with a more lively imagination and much more egotism than your mate. You believe that
the woman you choose, or are chosen by, is the most perfect
peach on the tree and probably the smartest, else why did she
seem to appreciate your charms above all others? Every man
knows that he is God's finest handiwork, and the woman who
realizes that fact must be wise indeed. Love, to her, is a way
of getting along in the world, fulfilling her destiny, boosting her
ego, paying for the pork chops, and avoiding the disgrace of
having "miss" written on her tombstone. It is a complicated
mess that no man will ever understand, and it is as different
from that which dwells in your breast as was Caruso from Elvis
Presley—truly a many splendored thing.

Woman conscientiously adorns herself in order to attract the
male creature. She thinks she knows exactly what he is looking
for, and does her mechanical best to set the trap and make the
bait appealing. And as long as she is going at this thing in such
a down to earth and practical way it behooves you to do a little
research before committing yourself. Unfortunately things are
not always what they seem, and it is my painful duty to destroy
some of your fond illusions, so in the future you cannot say the
doc didn't tell you.

Don't be overwhelmed by her show of passion and devotion
or you might wind up like an old friend of mine. He was a

widower and so should have known better, but fooling a man is like taking candy from a baby. He was going with a nice quiet little homebody when some other dame decided to cut in on the game. This vulture used all the shopworn tricks to convince him that he had swept her completely off her feet and that she was about to be consumed by the passions which he caused to flame up within her.

They were married, and three weeks later he was in my office with the following tale of woe. She wore a wig; she took seven kinds of vitamin and pep pills before going to bed, but they generated no romance. In the morning she consumed an hour making up her face and another half hour strapping on her breasts and hips. If he wanted any breakfast before going to work he had to prepare his own. She spit like a cat when he even touched her, only wore her false teeth when company was coming, and kept house like a pack rat.

Like most women of this type, she hugely enjoyed poor health and had insisted that he get a doctor for her. When he came to see me I suggested that he needed a kick in the pants for getting himself into such a mess, but he was a good friend and patient, so I agreed to examine his prize. The history was so long and involved that she seemed to have had all the diseases in the book. The scars upon her abdomen looked like a railroad map of Indiana with the navel as Indianapolis.

She gave me a note to her Salt Lake City physician authorizing him to brief me upon her medical experiences, and a few days later when I was in the city we went over the case together. She was twenty years older than the age given on her marriage certificate, had lost all her female organs plus one kidney, thyroid gland and gall bladder, and three previous husbands to boot. So many surgeons had been fooled by her grunting that it would seem that her belly must be stuffed with straw, since everything else had been removed.

I talked the matter over with the lady and her husband and advised that she was in such a delicate condition that living in our town was a great risk; she should be under the care of a specialist at all times, and should live in a much lower altitude, because of her heart. She had discovered that hubby was not as wealthy as she had supposed, so this gave her a wonderful excuse to suggest that if he would give her a hundred dollars she would grant him a divorce and move to California. It was a solution he was most happy to accept.

Back in Missouri we used to get rid of these chronic grunters by suggesting that they move to the Rocky Mountains. In Utah we sent them to Southern California, and I suppose the doctors there send them on to the islands, or suggest some new and weird religion to occupy their minds, as there are plenty of such in that neighborhood. Fortunately surgeons are not so knife-happy as they once were, and these poor unfortunate psychopaths eventually wind up where they belong, their minds occupied by novel and strange cults rather than the malfunctioning of their internal organs.

All women are most susceptible to any queer notions about their innards and just love to be suffering from some strange ailment that the other girls don't have. Medical articles in magazines for women do nothing to destroy this queer appetite.

It may sound harsh, but you must be practical and look this baby over as though you were buying a horse. The girl is mother of the woman, and *her* mother is the architect of the whole. If mother is a grunter and always sick and the girl resembles her in looks, manners and actions, she too will spend all your money in drug stores and hospitals. On the other hand, if she resents her mother's delicate health enough she is likely to follow in her dad's footsteps; he never had a chance to grunt in his whole married life, so she too will resist that greatest of feminine pleasures, going to the doctor.

Now that we have proved that your loved one is pretty much of a phony and that she has used tricks to ensnare you which a horse trader wouldn't use on a sucker, let's look at the other side of the bargain and see just what she is going to get for all of this trouble.

In the first place she does not approach marriage with the bull-like passion that sparks your own emotions. To her you are only a means to an end, and it is to her everlasting credit that once you have performed your biological function, she restrains her savage impulses and does not devour you, as the scorpion and the black widow spider devour their husbands. Secondly, she expects you to be able to support her while she is indulging in her primal function of bearing children and to keep her one step ahead of the neighbors in all the status symbols Vance Packard ever dreamed of.

To achieve all this she is willing to accept a lot poorer specimen than you are; you may be bowlegged, pot-bellied, bald-headed and smell like a pet shop on Monday morning, but still she swears that she loves you.

But beware of the feminine ingenuity. Look the merchandise over carefully before making your downpayment. Does she laugh at your jokes in the proper places? Mix her up and tell some with a sober face and avoid laughing at your own telling. That is perhaps a dirty trick, but it will divulge a sense of humor if there is any there.

Does she wipe her lips with a kleenex and then wad it up and drop it on the restaurant floor? If so, she will do the same in her own household and you will live in sweet confusion and litter the rest of your life.

Is her show of kindness toward children and dogs an act, or does she seem to be casual but adept in her approach to those barnacles that stick to the good ship matrimony?

Does she take an unusual interest in sports and claim to like hunting, fishing and roughing it? If so, she is either an accomplished liar or one of these masculine women that all men abhor.

Is she a cute little kitten with an appetite of an anaconda? If so, expect her to let all restraints go once she is married and look like an inflated balloon before she reaches forty.

When courting your pride and joy, you never see her with a hair out of place or a button missing, in fact she looks good enough to eat. Her parlor is neatness personified and if you stay for dinner you are led to believe that each meal is a state dinner with all the good silver and Limoges china a commonplace.

Wedded bliss will be somewhat different. Women just love to slop around in an old bathrobe, their hair wadded up under a frilly little cap and their feet encased in flat sandals which flop at every step. Billie Burke advises every woman to get up ten minutes before her man awakes, skip to the bathroom, make up her face, comb her hair and then crawl back in bed before she awakens the lord and master. She says she did it, but if so, she was a most remarkable woman and all alone in her glory. Most women look like something the cat dragged in until at least eleven o'clock in the morning. The picture the old man has in his mind to compare with the trim little stenographers who surround him all day is quite a contrast. Wifey looks okay when he gets home at night, but the damage is already done; he still remembers how she looked when he left that morning.

Let's survey the subject from head to foot and consider some of the other atrocities she has committed in the name of fashion.

I will acknowledge that the female form divine is much more likely to resemble the Venus de Milo than you do the Greek gods one sees in art museums, but do not try to endow her with all the charms that art and science would lead you to believe are hidden beneath that attractive gown. Investigate her yourself, and do not allow the TV advertising to mislead you.

For instance, women do not smell as badly as the commercials would have you believe, and all these deodorants and perfumes are not absolutely necessary if the lady is addicted to the use of soap and water. Like man himself, if she is careless about her hygiene, she stinks; clean, she is just as attractive without all these roll-ons and beauty aids as with them, and perhaps more so. I suspect they are used for the same purpose that trappers use scent on their traps—to snare the amorous-minded male fox.

Close inspection will reveal the eye shadow and false lashes she uses to give the soulful look. You already know just how badly lipstick, rouge and powder rub off on a man's shirt.

If she wears a lot of jewelry around her neck you can be sure she is hiding a few wrinkles. This is the spot where women first show their age; the older they get the more they look like picked chickens in a poultry market. And yet a clean and well-formed neck with an upswept hairdo stirs up the stallion in man more than any of his mate's more revealing charms.

Every woman wants to look exactly like every other woman and still appear to have a distinctive style all her own. Her hat and hair styles must be perfect copies of the prevailing models, yet if she sees the same headpiece on another woman's head, the attractiveness of her own is spoiled. The wearers of identical hats become mortal enemies with thoughts of mayhem toward each other.

You must learn to disregard women's hats and hairdos. You are too callous to understand the female motivation in regard to styles, and will probably remain in that state as long as you live. If you ever do figure out why she butchers her hair as she does, you can dismiss the Theory of Relativity as mere child's play—you are indeed the wisest of men.

When I was a medical student fifty years ago I naturally spent some time upon the wards of hospitals for the insane. It was customary, when a new patient was brought in, for the first nurse that saw her to whip out bandage shears and recklessly hack off the patient's hair just to get rid of it. If the woman was not crazy when committed, this insult to her womanly charm tipped the scales in insanity's favor. Some time and place in these later years a barber, who hated women, committed this crime upon the crowning glory of a prominent actress, and Bingo! all the girls blossomed out in wind-blowns, poodle cuts and other styles too horrible to describe. The end result looked like nothing familiar except a badly used mop. When my wife first came home wearing this new style I instinctively unloaded all my guns, hid the ammunition, dulled the butcher knives, chopped up the rolling pin and prepared for the worst. A doctor learns to be alert to any sudden changes in the behavior of his patients that might indicate a deranged mind.

Mother Nature intended woman's hair to be a soft, flattering frame for her face. Modern novelists to the contrary, this crowning glory is the first thing any man notices about a woman. Piled high on her head, it lends a look of dignity to a rather small and unattractively shaped skull. This hairdo also exposes the back of a woman's neck which, if reasonably slender, generates a desire to bite it. When woman chopped off her hair the Age of Chivalry died; if she now has to stand up in streetcars and light her own cigarettes, it's because her own sins are coming home to roost.

All the girls blossomed out in poodle cuts.

Now (may the girls forgive me) I must tell the truth; the anatomy lesson must reveal what's under all the camouflage. Art and science have fashioned brassieres and built-ins to create the illusion of loveliness; but careful investigation should be limited, except in the semi-darkness of a dimly lit room, where as the great Franklin discovered, all cats are gray. And if these cats confine their vocal efforts to purring instead of yowling and spitting, the deviations from the ideal conformation will not be noticed. In such circumstances all women are beautiful.

Now we will skip to the area of her hips, and dismiss this important region with one bald statement; women were not supposed to wear pants; if they are somewhat fat and broad of beam, it is a bigger crime than pushing baby chickens into the irrigation ditch. If they start an argument with hubby while wearing pants, his natural instincts will take over and he will swing one from the hip just as he would at any other pants-wearing animal.

And so to her feet. In flat-heeled shoes or barefoot sandals they appear much too big for the rest of her body, and such shoes have created more old bachelors than distaste for mothers-in-law. Therefore, although it is a crime against nature, we men are happy to accept high-heeled shoes. Not only do they make the feet appear more graceful, but wearing them contracts the muscles on the back of the leg and so gives that region a more attractive form, and a promise of shapeliness up beyond the range of our vision. But they sure play the devil with her toes.

When I was a child, our midwestern country was bled white every year by some missionary just returned from China. Her talking point was the horrible custom of binding little girl's feet so they would not grow along with the rest of her body. The ladies of the church worked themselves blind to raise money so the work of liberating these unfortunate females from bondage might progress, and yet they were doing the same thing to themselves in the interest of fashion.

Someday the evolutionary process will remodel women's feet so that there is only a hoof where the toes should be and the heel will be halfway up the leg, as in the cow and horse of today. But until that time comes, why must they paint their toenails the color of anemic blood? Toenail polish always reminds me of the feet of a mountain lion I once saw killed shortly after it had attacked a colt and torn it cruelly with the claws of its rear feet, while trying to give the death bite upon the animal's neck.

Woman manages, sometime between eleven o'clock in the morning and the end of hubby's working day, to commit all kinds of crimes upon her person. She seems to have little regard for her original self, which is truly a masterpiece of nature's handiwork. She forgets that a man is an imaginative creature, and leaves little room for him to exercise his powers along that line. With her hair piled on top of her head, in a becoming dress and high-heeled shoes she can indeed inspire wild visions of further loveliness. But I must nevertheless remind all you gullible males of the old adages: "Let the buyer beware." "Look before you leap!" "All that glitters . . ."

6

Can This Marriage
Be Avoided?

To GIVE YOU a basic understanding of the union of the sexes, let us turn our imaginations loose and thumb back the pages of romantic time to the beginning. In the second chapter of this book we made the point that the union of Adam and Eve was not a true marriage because they were of the same bone and flesh, and that Cain and the Nod girls began all this monkey business. We do not know just what the Nod females looked like. But we will suppose that the scene opens with them sitting about the roots of the family tree, gossiping, painting their lips and fingernails with poke berry juice, and cussing the guy who last arranged their hair. Suddenly a strange bellow breaks the quiet of the valley. Being wise to the ways of their world, they scamper up the tree to await the coming of this strange animal in comparative safety. Pretty soon here he comes, probably a hairy, apelike creature, his eyes red and blazing from the excitement of having just bumped off his brother, his lips stained a sickly orange with the pumpkin juice which the Lord had turned down in favor of lamb chops. Of course he is roaring and cussing as does any other frustrated male, and all in all is a bargain that even Eve probably would have disowned.

"What in the world is that thing?" queries one of the sisters who is peeping down through the foliage at this grotesque monster.

"Maybe it's a man," answers the youngest and dumbest of the family.

"Don't be ridiculous. Nobody would dare go near that thing unless she wanted to be killed at once."

But the little dumb Dora is still young enough to have married Sam Levenson's bear without thinking about the possible consequences, so she climbs down to the lower branches for a better look.

"Well, I'm going to find out; I don't want to be an old maid and I *do* want to be an ancestor, so it's worth the risk." With that she plucks an apple, cocoanut, or whatever, and taking careful aim beans the brute with this love missile.

Cain, of course, looks up to see who is attacking him, and with a mighty roar swarms up the tree after his tormentor. She

Taking careful aim, she beans the brute with a love missile.

can out-run, out-climb or out-last this big hulking brute at any time, but today she is unusually awkward. As she climbs up she also slips back, giving him the illusion that his mighty power and agility are sure to overcome her. Just as he is about to grasp one pretty little ankle, she seemingly loses all holds upon the tree and falls back into his arms, throwing hers about his neck and screaming, "Save me."

Having such an unusually soft and yielding body draped upon his chest upsets the brute's balance; they would both fall to the ground but for the fact that as she falls she prudently hooks one knee over a stout limb, and thus anchored, holds both of them safely against the trunk. As planned Cain is not aware of this anchor to windward and thinks that it is his own agility that saved them a nasty bump. Now that this soft little creature is depending upon him to save her from harm, by golly he will do just that. So he climbs carefully down the tree and tenderly carries her out into the wilderness, where like Eve before her, she reveals to him that fact that he is a boy and she is a girl. And she has no snake to advise her, either. So she gets her wish and becomes the mother of a good part of the human race. Enoch was her first son.

When Seth showed up in this neighborhood the females of Nod were raining down on him like hickory nuts in a windstorm, and so Enos arrived to help Enoch populate earth. By the time poor old Solomon came on the scene the technique was so perfected that he had rescued a thousand damsels before he realized that he was the patsy in this game of you-chase-me-until-I-catch-you.

Being a patsy for women came naturally to poor old Solomon; any son of David and Bathsheba was bound to inherit some queer ideas about love and marriage. When we look at an old stallion like Solomon and compare him with modern man, we can better understand the slogan of the *Ladies Home Journal*, "Never underestimate the power of a woman." Anthropologists would have us believe that Cain differed from the apes only in having an opposing thumb, eyes that could focus, and a cranial bump of curiosity. Perhaps he was not a handsome

specimen, but he gave forth an aroma and appearance of masculinity strong enough to charm a Nod maiden out of a tree.

Could a modern man, walking down that forest trail so long
ago, have done as well? From her tree the Nod maiden would
have beheld a baldheaded, clean-shaven, pot-bellied little
squirt wearing plastic-rimmed spectacles, his mouth full of
safety pins, a dishtowel draped over one shoulder, a diaper in
his hand, and muscles so poorly developed he would have to
tip the bellboy to get assistance carrying his bride over the
threshold of his honeymoon hotel. The maiden would probably
have fallen out of her tree all right, but it would have been
because of laughter rather than any irresistible urge to mate
with such a creature. The power of women accomplished this
horrendous transformation; when the descendants of the Nod
maidens started to civilize the male, they succeeded in damn
near wrecking him.

It was ordained that man, in his gestation period, should go
through all the steps of ages of evolution; he begins as a tad-
pole, then a fish and so on until millions of years of progress is
compressed into a period of nine months. But one thing never
changes; he still falls for that old badger game. Beaned on the
head with an apple, a sly glance, a glimpse of a shapely leg as
she climbs the tree, the pursuit, the capture, the steadying influence of that leg hooked over a limb; delusions of mastery,
children, mortgages, swimming pools, taxes and all the rest of
the things that go to make up our civilization. We fondly think
that we have made progress from that first eventful day in Nod,
but we have done so only in ways that make the woman's life
less strenuous and more exciting. Man himself can never hope
to improve upon his own lot. He is still a frustrated though
shaven ape, charging about the earth trying to evade the curse
of Cain and to secure forgetfulness and peace of mind; yet he
vents his lust for retail or wholesale murder upon his fellows
and prays in public for peace on earth, good will to men.

If that Nod maiden had just let well enough alone and
stayed up in that tree, what a peaceful world this would have
been. But no; like her daughters of today, she took the risk of

taming this half-wild ape. Even though experience has taught these later women that the offspring will turn out little better than their distant ancestor, still they don't drown the male babies but cherish them.

Stop for just a minute, fellows, and think back about what your wife will have to endure over the years, and you will understand the devious workings of her mind a little better. It is indeed fortunate that there is more than physical passion involved in her choice of a mate; she knows you are no bargain, but generations of female ancestors have bequeathed her a certain adroitness in handling this unreasonable creature and she feels sure that she can cope with your eccentricities better than with those of some other man. She comes to you prepared to assume the minor role, and to at least appear to obey your every insane command. She accepts the role of a dependent and has to spend half her life thinking up ways to separate you from enough of your money to keep her offspring and herself dressed properly and well fed. She has to smooth out your rough spots that you may appear semi-civilized when out in public. As Longfellow so aptly put it, "she leads you, yet she follows." Which, come to think of it, is some accomplishment in itself.

I know my own life better than any other man's, and what my wife had to endure. She married a man who tried to dominate her every action, a brute of most uncertain disposition who got mad and threw things upon the least provocation. Added to that she had a family of boys who showed all the natural male characteristics and were a trial to a mother who longed for a daughter that would be a kindred spirit. She had a burning desire to travel and see the world, and a stubborn old goat for a husband who wouldn't go anyplace that he could not drive himself. She is an excellent cook who loves to dream up new dishes and I want mush twice a day and pot roast the other meal 364 days out of 365.

I feel that I am a paragon among husbands, but I realize that there are times when my pride and joy is justified in a feeling of frustration and disappointment. Once the boys were raised,

she hoped and expected to settle down to a comfortable existence with her friends in familiar surroundings. But I yanked
her out of this peaceful life, moved to a strange state, and
forced her to become a farmer's wife with all the chores this
implies, just because I wanted to live a few years by the sweat
of my brow instead of other people's misfortunes.

In this the last act, I am closeted away in my den pecking
on a typewriter all morning. She spends most of the afternoon
reading aloud what I have written, and if perchance she looks
up from the manuscript this is what she sees: An old man
wrinkled and grey, slumped down in his big chair sound asleep;
his hair on end, his mouth partly open, dressed in sox, pants
and undershirt, the latter covered with pipe ashes from the
pipe which has slipped down into his lap. His glasses and a
complete set of artificial dentures are grinning at her from the
smoking stand. And yet she claims to love me.

That's one wife for you. Now let's look at your own intended.

She has singled you out from the herd of male prospects, and
though she has as yet no legal claims upon you, still she has
you bull-eyed in her sights. Once she is able to forget the ideal
prince charming of her maidenly dreams, she will pull the trig-
ger and one more recruit is lost to bachelorhood.

She expects to assume your name, and if this simple require-
ment was on the other foot you would be damned if you would
follow through with it. You wouldn't change your name and so
your identity to marry a hundred women like her. Also she expects you to be the head of the family in actions as well as
name; she will hold a minor and supporting role all through
life, and she is most unhappy if it doesn't work out that way.
She hopes to civilize you a bit and make you presentable to her
friends and will brag about you with her last breath, that she
may make the other girls envious. She is confident that she can
remake you into the sort of man she hoped to find in the first
place. And she has to do all of this by adroitness rather than
with a club.

Just why does she pick you? Ask her, and if she is truthful
her answer will likely be, "God only knows." But there was a

time when she thought she did know, and one of the following prerequisites is probably the reason you're about to find yourself in a state of wedded bliss.

1. Love—she will swear that love (actually she means the sex urge) is the principal motivation for her catastrophic behavior, but she is beyond the teen-age phase when love is everything.
2. Conformity—all the other girls are getting married and she doesn't want to be left hanging on the limb.
3. Security—a bank account and a good job of her own aren't enough.
4. Glamor and status—when status and love are adversaries, love is a one to twenty shot to win. I once had a short but violent romance with a tall stately nurse from Iowa. We were not serious; I didn't want a statue of Liberty and she already had two potential scalps she could hang from her belt. One was a Greek God of a man, but he was poor and a farmer; the other was a little shrimp of a physician. She intended to foreclose on the doc because, as she said, "When I drive down Michigan Boulevard in my Cadillac, nobody will know that my husband's hair tickles my nose when we dance."
5. The fun of stealing some other girl's mate, or the fear that some snake might get away with her own intended if she does not bind him legally at once.
6. Boredom and loneliness (of panic proportions after twenty-five).
7. The natural female desire to keep house and care for some man.
8. The simple fact that getting married has been held up as her goal since babyhood, and she does not want to be regarded as a miserable failure by parents and friends. After all, there has been a lot of time and money spent preparing her for this momentous event, and she feels that it should not be wasted.
9. The sense of accomplishment and the thrill of being

the center of the stage for one day at least. When she struts down the aisle with her quarry waiting at the altar, she experiences the same thrill you do when you hold up the biggest fish for the photographer.
10. The fact that you are the only fairly eligible man handy when the nesting urge becomes dominant.

I have left out the basic urge to upbreed with a superior male that the offspring may be an improvement upon the root stock because it is obvious that she must compromise with that primal instinct when she decides to marry you. But she has made her decision, and like the judges in a prize contest, that decision is final. If you would avoid the successful culmination of this enterprise you had better take it on the lam right now; if you stay home and welsh on the arrangements you are a cad, despised by all females and laughed at by your male friends.

Just why we males allow our wives to inculcate the idea of marriage into the male children, I do not know. Life would be so simple if this relationship could be avoided. Yet what man who has ever been married would hesitate to take on the yoke again if opportunity offered? It's like the old tale about the child hitting his thumb with a hammer, stating that he did it simply because it felt so good when he stopped. Marriage will continue as an institution as long as women desire it, simply because the male is too susceptible to her wiles to avoid it.

All men are faced with much the same problem as told to me by a Japanese labor boss before World War I when picture brides were contraband. He sent a list of specifications to the old country and in return received pictures of maidens who would consider coming to America to be his wife. He made his choice and then was informed that the initial expense would include outfitting the bride for the trip and hiring three witnesses who would swear that she was already his lawful wedded wife. This took a lot of money: she needed twenty silk kimonos and, because he had left the old country a year or two before she was born, some pretty imaginative and hence expensive witnesses. When she arrived in San Francisco the U.S. Immigration Service got nosy again, and he needed three more good brothers, at stateside prices, to swear that they had known both parties when they were wedded in Japan.

"Doc," he said to me just before she arrived, "I've got four thousand dollars invested in this deal already, and I have no idea what kind of a woman I'm going to get. The cost is enormous and the risk is great, but we've just got to have wives, regardless of worry and expense."

We men are susceptible, and sometimes even desperate, although we don't often have the guts of my Japanese friend to admit it. Such being the case, it behooves us old chaps that are nearing port without too many disastrous ship wrecks to chart the course we have traveled for those that may come after us.

Now we will suppose that she has swallowed the line you have been feeding her about love forever true, Cadillacs and a villa on the Riviera plus moonlight every night. Because or in spite of all this romantic sales talk, among other things, she has decided to take your name and be your ever-loving wife. She has visions of a big production of course, for this her day of fulfillment; it will probably cost as much as a modest cottage.

You have no such ambitions and would gladly drop by the office of a Justice of the Peace and go through the rites before two hired witnesses. But take care or you may end up like the couple who applied to a near-sighted old Justice of the Peace to be married during the deer hunting season. He took their two dollars, issued a license and married them. After they left he discovered he had issued a hunting license, not a marriage license, so he rushed down the street after them yelling, "If you ain't done it, don't do it! That paper ain't for it!"

But your hope of sneaking off quietly will not be considered in this matter; her mother has been planning for this event ever since the child was born, and brought her up to expect such a blowout to be her birthright. They have been ganging up on the old man ever since the girl decided that you were the best she could hope for in the lottery of lifetime mates, and he has mortgaged the farm and prepared himself for the worst; namely living with you in his old age.

Here is a spot where, if you use your head, you may be able to save yourself some money and keep the old man solvent.

Make a date to meet him in some bar downtown and suggest that he develop a fierce dislike toward you and make his feelings known around the house. If he is a good enough actor he can swear he will shoot you rather than have his little chickadee married to such a brute. Caution him to find the right story to use in this little deception; if he will swear that he understands that you are a wild one, with seven or more little social errors running about the town that look like you, it will in no way lessen your intended's affection, but make her more determined to cut this wild stallion out of the herd and domesticate him.

For your own part, act crushed by his actions and beg of her that she fly away with you just to spite him. She, being a female, will probably do just that. This kind of a wedding yields unexpected dividends; the old man will show himself noble and forgiving and offer to come and live with you anyhow; if so you always have a blackmailer's dream to keep him in line. You have saved money, will not be dogged silly by having your wife drag out that faded wedding dress and weep gently for the dreams she had while wearing it and the disappointments she has accumulated since. And your granddaughters will bless you because they will have no old-fashioned dress bequeathed to them that they must wear on their wedding day.

If your intended papa-in-law seems shocked at the proposition and swears that he would never dream of such perfidy, you have him catalogued; either he is a monumental liar or such a poor stick that he lets his female relations do his thinking for him. If this gal was brought up in that kind of an atmosphere you had better think twice before carrying out your part of the contract; she will expect to handle you the same way her mother got the hammerlock on the old man.

Should all these schemes fail and you are forced to wear the gay plumage of groom-to-be, plus the sad sweet mannerisms of an undertaker, take heart. It will only last half an hour and nobody will notice your presence anyhow. At a wedding the groom serves the same function as the frame in which the picture is displayed. His use is simply to draw attention to the queen of the occasion. And remember this is probably the last time her father will be furnishing the drinks and chicken sandwiches, so cheer up; eat, drink and be merry because you know not of the morrow.

And tomorrow will present queer and unusual problems. You cannot get up in the morning, don your raiment and bid your night's companion a pleasant good morning as of yore. Old habits are hard to break; watch yourself—dress but do not put on your hat until she is ready to go out to breakfast. Soon enough you will both realize that you are two incompatible elements poured into the test-tube of matrimonial bliss. We hope that the resultant chemical reaction expends itself by causing a few harmless bubbles to spill over the top of the test tube, and not an H-bomb explosion that will leave scars upon both of you for the rest of your natural lives.

She saw a new recipe.

The very first thing you must train yourself to do is grab the daily paper and sit on it until you have had time to digest the stock market page and the sports section. Someone has said that a woman reads a newspaper as if she were eating an artichoke; she devours the base of each leaf and discards the rest upon the floor in a disorganized pile. That man was a keen observer. No man can ever rearrange a newspaper once his wife has had her hands on it, and if after an hour's effort he does get it into a semblance of order he will find great holes right in the middle of the market listings or the funny pages. She saw a new recipe for making coffee without boiling water and she tore it out and filed it on her desk where she will never look at it again.

Try and be as gentle with your new wife as your temperament will permit, which probably isn't saying much, you being a man. She has even greater problems of adjustment than you ever thought of; her big day is behind her and there is no gloom equal to that engendered by the knowledge that one's time in the limelight has passed, and that from here on out she will be known as Mrs. Somebody-else, her own individualism a thing of the past. A girl can only be a bride once; she may get married a dozen times but the glamor is all gone, "the captains and the kings depart" once she reaches the chapel door on her way out the first time.

Besides, she is suddenly overcome with a new worry—one that will dog her every waking moment for the next thirty years. *Is* she or *ain't* she? Try and imagine just how you would react if, for twenty-five days out of thirty, you were constantly wondering whether or not a strange individual was taking form within you. The suspense would make a gibbering idiot of you within three months. To complicate matters, half the time she hopes it is so and the other half she knows that she will just die if it proves to be a fact.

On top of all this, she has to adjust her life and actions to avoid clashes with the most unpredictable and unstable creature that ever lived on earth, a strange man. Regardless of the pangs you endure, her lot is many times as trying.

That is why nature begins to condition her soon after birth; now all the little subterfuges and equivocations she learned as a child come in handy. For one thing she has got to make you believe that she is a virgin; that you are the first man she ever even kissed and that she thinks you're wonderful. Ordinary gumption makes you know that this line is probably as phony as a three dollar bill, but man must believe that story or there is something lost in the family relationship. No man is going to feel that he must protect and cherish some dame who has been cherished by a half dozen other males. If she was a widow, okay, but if "Miss" was on her calling card when you met her she just must be as pure as a lily that had never seen a bee, as inexperienced as when she was two years old, and never attracted to any other male except her father.

You won't get that kind of a freak, but you once believed in Santa Claus and you will bring all of those old powers of imagination to the front again and convince yourself that she is brand new merchandise never handled by other shoppers, and that the last twenty years have been spent in just preparing herself to be the mate of such a paragon of virtue as you. And if she is a wise young lady she will nourish that vision with all her inborn female guile, but it puts a mighty strain even upon a woman's intelligence, having to act like a sexual moron all the time clear up to the age of seventy. A happy marriage is based upon illusions, and the dame who can keep those same hallucinations growing well in your head is a successful wife.

You have to make some adjustments too, but you don't have to lie about your experiences with her sex. You may be accused of bragging about your way with girls, but she expects to get somewhat damaged and shopworn affections and pays little attention to your tales of past exploits.

There are several things that you should understand about this newly acquired partner of your joys and sorrows and the most important is the sexual, of course. First, unlike you, she is not always in the mood for love. Like the female of all animals, when she is governed by this mood she requires more attention than you are physically able to supply, and when not in the mood—to hell with it, she only accepts your show of affection to save a fuss. Try and keep the fact ever ready for reference in that thick skull of yours that she was made for an entirely different purpose than you, constructed in a weird and peculiar fashion, and that no man can ever understand just what forces are motivating her actions. As Eugene Field so aptly put it in speaking about boys, "They never had been mothers and could never hope to be."

We cannot do without women, we cannot hope to understand them, and we definitely cannot make them into males, even though the educators in our schools seem bent upon doing so. They may assume some of men's prerogatives, but if they become too much like men they lose their womanhood and so their attractiveness. As a woman despises a sissyfied male, so do men shun a woman who thinks and acts like a man.

Woman is, as all men will agree, never satisfied with anything, and that includes husbands; there is always the thought lingering in her subconscious that if she had married some other man life might have been more glamorous. Most women are quite successful in keeping this disappointment under wraps, but I have known many a woman who goaded her husband to distraction by forever reminding him that she could have lived a more glamorous life with someone else.

Do not let this get you down. Instead of trying to get the moon for her, tell her that you wish to hell she had been successful in landing that other guy because you have seen much nicer looking fruit on the market since you picked this slightly withered and shop-worn peach. You would be equally happy if the marriage contract had contained a clause allowing one to return the merchandise within sixty days if not found to be just as advertised. But you are nevertheless stuck with each other till death or infidelity do you part.

Whenever I see a young couple just joined in wedlock going out to face the world together, I regret that I do not have the power to transform them into ignorant savages upon some tropical island where the past is forgotten, the present tranquil, and the future only a misty dream. The Creator intended that His children should live in the Garden of Eden, enjoy each day to its fullest, and spend no time in thought of the tomorrows. And if ever there is a time in people's lives when they should drink from this cup prepared for them by the Allwise, it is the honeymoon years.

But man, in his eternal quest for the golden fleece, has destroyed the possibilities of even this tiny respite from the treadmill of progress and is chained thereon until old age and decrepitude overtake him. Then it is too late to enjoy anything.

Shaw said, "Youth is wonderful, it's too bad that it is wasted on young people." He should have said that it is unfortunate that we elders have set up such false standards to which young people must conform that they have no time to enjoy their birthright. You who are embarking upon this journey will find that your days are so crowded with worries, frustrations, and insane demands that you have little time to enjoy the pleasure of each other's company.

For some cockeyed reason it is an unwritten law in our society that the newly married couple must begin life together surrounded by all the conveniences and gadgets that their parents took fifty years of hard work to acquire. "A jug of wine and thou singing beside me in the wilderness" may be paradise, but very few brides would be satisfied with anything less than champagne and a cottage furnished like a luxury hotel. This puts the burden of debt upon your already sagging shoulders and the worst of it is, before you get the damned stuff paid for, she throws it all away and refurnishes in the style of this year's hotels. Some other girl has a mink coat and if you loved your own sweetie you would grab a club and rush out into the wilds of Wilshire Boulevard and knock over a few mink and minkesses that you might provide her with this most necessary of status symbols. She will never wear it, but it looks so nice draped over her arm.

But let's get back to more earthy things than fur coats. For the first week she enjoyed washing by hand the few dishes she used, but then she heard about dishpan hands, and "Bang!" she had to have a dishwasher, and a combination washer and dryer for the laundry. She can do your washings at the laundromat for three years for what the washer cost, and in that time the old thing is shot anyhow and you have to buy a new one. At the laundromat you save the carrying charge, repair bills and two hundred dollars' worth of soap.

If you have to use the car to go to work she has to have a brand new one, because surely you wouldn't want your precious to get corns on her feet walking a block to the supermarket, and only people with dirty work clothes use the busses.

She must have colored telephones in every room just in case the house catches on fire, and she uses them at least five full hours a day, gassing with her girl friends. This is time well spent because in this way she hears of all the new gadgets some other man's wife has acquired and has time to think up reasons why you should buy her one, on your way home.

She finds out just what you like to eat the first month you are married, but three times out of five she serves up some mess for dinner which was featured in a popular magazine along with pretty pictures of a beautiful model explaining how this particular dish made gracious living more gracious. Other nights you get a frozen TV dinner fresh from the oven of that brand new three hundred dollar cook stove. The biscuits were made at a bakery three weeks ago and go under the name of "brown and serve." The cake was mixed by Betty Crocker or Duncan Hines and a five-year-old could read the directions and serve it just as nicely as she can. The bread comes in a cellophane wrapper and is full of junk to keep it fresh. Frozen peas and carrots are so much nicer because she does not have time or inclination to shell or wash the real articles. And the state probably spent three or four thousand dollars of tax money teaching her domestic science in high school.

If all this gets you down she rushes out and gets a job. Now you get TV dinners *every* night, dinners so alike in taste and appearance that you have to look at the label on the package to know what you are eating. Now you also need a maid to come in and care for the house, extra clothes for the wife to wear at the office, and aspirin for the headaches she gets there. All you get is conversation devoted to the males she comes in contact with during business hours, and a wife who is too tired to appreciate your show of affection either before or after going to bed.

By practicing such economies as cutting your own hair and wearing paper soles in your shoes you think maybe in three months you will be up on your monthly payments enough to buy a new shirt. Just then somebody gets careless and she begins to talk about the patter of little feet. Of course this is the real reason you got married, but the shock almost kills most fathers. Bills, bills, bills. Statistical graphs tell us that seventy per cent of broken marriages are caused by money matters, in other words, debts from installment buying and impossible bills that must be met somehow. And whose fault is it? Not yours; and surely and emphatically not hers! She is so equipped by nature that she could get along nicely and rear her young successfully in a cave situated above snow and timber line.

That Nod strain was made of a lot tougher stuff than poor old Adam; he was brought up in the Garden where he had nothing to do but name animals while the Nod folks had to scratch for a livelihood from the beginning. Consequently, though your little wife loves luxury, her inheritance endowed her with a body and mind much more active than your own, and an ability to endure hardships (and thrive thereon) which would kill you in a week. And strange as it may seem, if she is forced by circumstances to revert to the status of a cave woman she will, down deep in her heart, enjoy the experience.

I took my bride to a mining camp where the only modern convenience we possessed was a gasoline lantern; we slept in a tent that was often covered with snow a foot deep, and did she have a good time! She would dance all night to music made by one drunken fiddler, and gossip with a bunch of Indian women who smelled so much like sage brush burning that I couldn't breathe around them. She was chased by rabid coyotes, and knocked around in train derailments, but not once did I ever hear her complain. Of course she expected to get out of there in a year or two, but she saw no reason to miss the fun of the experience.

So we can't place the blame for all these marriages that go to pieces on the rocks of debt and disappointment. Just whom can we convict? Not these poor kids who have to suffer from a bringing-up that in no way prepared them for life with all of its ups and downs. Nor can we place too much blame on their parents for raising them this way. Few parents were or are Spartan enough to deny their children the common comforts which they themselves enjoy. Can it be the schools who teach girls housekeeping chores in modern kitchens that cost more than all the rest of the laboratories in the plant put together? We insist that our little girls have all the advantages, even if the only thing they learn is to turn switches and steer vacuum cleaners. They get married without ever having seen a wash-board, a broom, or dishrag, believing that chickens come already picked and dressed, and that baking pans are something in which you place rocks, bulbs, and water so you can have extra early spring flowers blooming in the house.

The husband never walked a foot in his life except from the base to the dugout when he got caught napping on second. In all probability he never saw a lawn mower that needed pushing or a pile of wood to be cut for the fireplace. Both these innocents got most of their education from TV commercials, and commercials are designed by experts to make people want a particular product. That is our way of life: keep them dissatisfied with their lot so they will discard what they have and buy newer models and different products. This is our wonderful free enterprise system: keep everybody in debt paying for things he does not really need, and when he gets too old to hold a job keep him on social security or old age assistance. This year the two combined will cost the taxpayers close to twenty billion dollars, so we must increase the turnover, become more wasteful and unhappy with our transportation and furnishings, go farther in debt that we may support the old folks and make it next to impossible for a man to save enough to help himself after his sixtieth birthday. And we have the unmitigated gall to demand that other nations adopt our own way of life before we will give them a few crusts of bread that we do not need.

But back to our young married people, and whom to blame for the predicament in which we find them a couple of years after the ceremony which united them in these holy bonds. We are all to blame, and yet none of us are. It is a virus in our blood and can, I think, be credited to our Maker. He so constructed man and his brain that he would advance at an ever faster pace to accomplish the destruction of everything worth living for, and finally in a grand burst of Wagnerian music destroy man himself, his works and all the knowledge and culture which he so painfully created. His temples will crumble to dust and all trace of them will be covered by the sands of time.

And our children are still struggling even onward like salmon, braving the dams and obstructions of man's handiwork that they may propagate in familiar waters. How wonderful it would have been if we could have granted them just five years of absolute savagery that they might have enjoyed the world and all its beauties without knowledge of the mess that would fill their future.

Once you have taken the fatal steps to the altar you have no right to expect your wife to live in harmony with her mother-in-law if they are confined under the same roof, or even in the same town. Your mother-in-law may side with you just because you are a man, but even that close association is covered with barnacles on the good ship matrimonial-bliss. That old toast "To our wives and sweethearts, may they never meet" should have had "mothers" substituted for "sweethearts" and it would have had more meaning. Whistler's mother looked sad and forlorn sitting alone, but she had had her life and probably lived it as she wished. Each generation has its right to a time in the sun of opportunity. Maybe the old man did give your mother a rough go; but she made her choice in that dim past, and if he turned out to be a tramp don't make your kids suffer for the sins or ignorance of their grandmothers.

I am egotistical enough to believe that I married the best possible wife and mother for my children. She babied our boys something awful, but as they grew up she gradually retired and referred them to their pop with their troubles. When they got married she figuratively told them to scat, and as a consequence has always enjoyed the most pleasant relations with her daughters-in-law. When grandpa gets vexed and expresses a desire to spank a grandchild, she cools me down with a suggestion that I mind my own business. Unfortunately a lot of women are not so constituted, and grandmothers are more of a menace to happy family life than all the sirens that bothered poor Errol Flynn could ever be. Women are naturally very possessive regarding their male offspring, and it is most difficult for most mothers to accept another woman as a son's shining light, but it is nature's way and tears and reproaches will not alter it.

In our modern society, the effects women have on men are many and varied. The medicine has not been made that will counter the effects a nagging wife has upon her spouse, and there are more ulcers contracted at the breakfast table than at the office with all of its mad rush and anxieties. It is the constant dropping of water that wears away the stone, not the gush of a sudden flood that is forgotten tomorrow. May I repeat: many a good man is lost to the world because of a dissatisfied wife, and many a mutton-headed dolt is made to appear a wise and successful member of society because he was lucky enough to be married to a good woman.

If you don't find yourself a paragon of a woman, but rather find yourself stuck with a schemer, I must warn you that this vixen may have a tape recorder hidden behind a flower pot and a doctored tape can make things seem like what they aren't. Another accepted procedure today is for her to consult some psychoanalyst and have him discover some hidden fear or inhibition within her subconscious mind, caused by living with you, which generates much mental anguish. So she drags you into court and takes the shirt off your back in a settlement, of which her attorney gets half, and saddles you with court-ordered alimony which will keep your nose to the grindstone until she finds another male whose horoscope seems to blend more nicely with hers. We will never know just why living with a man for two or three years makes a perfectly capable female into a helpless sponge that requires her former spouse to keep her in the style she desires until she can catch another sucker. I believe a lot of women deserve a divorce as well as a settlement based upon what they had contributed to the union. I would even accept sexual contact, at two dollars per performance, balancing this sum against her personal upkeep during the wedded period, and add maid's wages if she kept the house. In other words, the final settlement, in many cases, would resolve itself into a good swift kick.

But if you married at nineteen or twenty, by the time she begins to show her claws there are two or three helpless little ones to consider and if you are a man you accept their responsibility and carry on, even though you are married to the old scratch herself.

Mr. Dooley once said that he planned to write a book of

laws, and on the first page there would be a statement to clarify the mode of enforcing them. It would read, "These laws mean what they mean and not what they say." If you intend to run your domestic establishment on a business-like basis, you had better follow the advice I gave husbands in another book and get a tape recorder before you buy a bed.

"Inconsistency, thy name is woman" is a statement of fact, and one of the things that make it possible for us males to live with women and to love them. The world would be a pretty boring old place if we did not have women to stir it up now and then with some ideas which, though in no way practical, still somehow make life happier and more interesting.

7

Quite Awfully Damned Contrary

Such, Polly, are your sex—part truth, part fiction;
Some thought, much whim, and all contradiction.
RICHARD SAVAGE

Woman is the only oxygen breathing creature on earth that is contrary and disorganized by natural choice. Man, along with the rest of the animals, becomes emotionally disturbed if life does not go along in the familiar manner; woman goes half crazy with boredom if it *does.*

If you change the time of feeding or the composition of the mash, a cow gets excited and fails to deliver the usual amount of milk; if you change the feed, chickens stop laying eggs; if a man is used to fried eggs and hotcakes for breakfast and is served some other combination, he gets indigestion. But if his mate is forced to do two things twice the same way, she is fit to be tied.

Let us consider the chore of feeding the family. A man would sit down the first day of the week and figure out a menu for the following seven days; he would not change the order of things from June to January except to substitute the vegetables in season for those in short supply. This would take all the worry and drudgery out of preparing meals. But will a woman consider such a well-ordered plan of existence? Hardly.

She prefers to walk into the kitchen half an hour before mealtime with her mind an absolute blank and trust her inspiration to guide her actions in preparing a meal. If there is a more complicated way of serving the supplies available, she will use it; if she doesn't know one she will pore over the cookbooks until she finds it. Your favorite dinner may be Boston brownbread and beans with pig knuckles, but if the scales showed her having gained a pound in the last week you will eat RYE-KRISP and lettuce salad, and for dessert some calorie-free pudding that tastes like smog.

She knows the things you like to eat and what agrees with you better than you do, but she considers that day lost that she does not try some recipe clipped from a woman's magazine, the results of which would knock the works out of a stone crusher if dumped into it. Belch loud and long, particularly if there is company present, and suffer pains of great intensity even if you have to make them up, and she won't repeat the outrage until the next month's issue arrives.

When one woman tries to tell another her recipe for as simple a thing as applesauce, Einstein would be confused if he tried to follow the directions. A little pinch of this and just enough of that, and on and on to infinity. Recipes are just inspirational suggestions to be modified at her whim—they have no relation to the specific directions used by men in creating anything.

They say that nothing gives a woman such a lift as the purchase of a new hat; the more hideous and unbecoming it is the more kick she gets out of it. Don't say what you think about the monstrosity; she knows it looks like the devil and that's the reason she bought it, believing that you would be more willing for her to purchase another one next week.

Now purchases, from hats to groceries, bring up a facet in the female mind and personality that is guaranteed to drive her male companion crazy should he be too often exposed to it. Women's actions while shopping have caused more fights and consequent automobile wrecks than booze. Nothing so infuriates a man as to have his wife spend a whole day in the stores, and nothing makes her madder than to have him try to hurry her when she has a nice, leisurely shopping trip in mind.

Your wife can go into the supermarket with the stated intention of buying a bottle of milk and a box of crackers and come out with fifteen dollars' worth of groceries and swear that they are all things that she needs to keep starvation from your door for the next two days. She may have the very same items squirreled away at home, but nevertheless she might run out of them sometime when she just has to have a jar of stuffed olives or some hummingbird tongues to garnish the salad she might make if there are any leftovers from dinner. And of course this chore of picking up the milk and crackers, which would have taken a man five minutes, takes her an hour, most of which she spends walking down the aisles looking at the pictures on the cans.

If for some reason you should accompany her to a department store, buy a couple of paperback books, rush off to the men's lounge and prepare yourself to spend the day. If she insists that she will call for you in an hour you can just as well go out to lunch and a picture show (even a double feature); you will still have an hour to wait after you return. But regardless of the time she spends, there is no need to worry about her driving you into bankruptcy; in all probability she will only have a new set of hair curlers to show for her full day's search, but she will have had a good time "shopping."

When a man goes into a store to buy a necktie he looks over the display in the case, picks out one or two that strike his fancy, compares them, picks one, pays for it and leaves. From his wife's viewpoint such actions border on the idiotic. She looks at every tie in the case and finally after an hour's careful examination tells the salesman that there is nothing that comes quite up to the style she had in mind.

Shoe stores are even worse. A woman suffers untold misery trying to kid herself and the salesman that every shoe he offers her is much too large, and she loves the man who will tell her that the nine EEE which fits her foot is a four AAA, and that only a few women have a foot narrow enough to wear this last.

It's a funny thing that women prefer other women as sales persons for all articles except shoes. The girls love to be lied to about their delicate tootsies and they know a lady clerk is mentally comparing their pedal extremities to duck feet. They just cannot tolerate untruthful women, even though they know there is no other kind.

These female shopping rambles are about as serious to a male as his fishing trips are to his wife. If he is smart he can avoid these aimless wanderings by having "business commitments" which mercifully keep him out of department stores and so enjoy a fair amount of immunity. But when a chap gets old and is retired he becomes a most vexing problem for his wife. If she parks him somewhere, he is likely to follow any strange female who gives him a pat on the head and a kind word, so his wife may have to look for him at the lost and found desk. But if she takes him along from counter to counter and floor to floor the day is spoiled for both of them.

I have often tricked my own wife into making an exact statement before we set out for the items she hopes to purchase during a shopping spree, and then by fast foot work and careful management succeeded in rounding up all of them by eleven A.M. I do this by getting her started early in the morning; clerks are fresh and eager to make a sale, and soon her list is complete. This does not mean that we go home, however; a time or two I have succeeded in dragging her to the car kicking and screaming, but most often I wind up in the park or the men's lounge with a book.

The latter place is not a cheerful spot. Half a dozen old coots sit around, their faces a blank until they hear the click of a woman's heels on the floor outside. Then they assume expressions of hope and anticipation for a moment, but when the heel taps go right on by that dog-waiting-for-his-master look comes back with a rush and they mentally return to scratching fleas.

It was just such male behavior that so impressed me with the canine cast to man's personality. If you do not believe that Adam descended from the canine strain, just drop into a men's lounge of a big department store and look over the specimens waiting there. Poodles, greyhounds, fox terriers and mastiffs—you will find them all tied to posts, hopefully waiting for their mistresses to return so they can wag their tails or growl, according to their condition of servitude.

Stand up for your rights and avoid shopping whenever you can. But if you can't, either get it over with in the early morning, or set out at about 4:30 on a day when the stores don't stay open late. It's more hectic this way, but the stores themselves will quickly save you by locking their doors.

The ordinary shopping trip, as I noted earlier, won't leave you bankrupt, but there's one kind of shopping that may. Beware of the home furnishing, furniture buying spree. Woman is continually dissatisfied with her surroundings, which is probably just as well—otherwise we would still be living in caves. But no matter how much time she spends choosing the decorations for your house, within a month after they are installed they are all wrong, and she is most unhappy until it comes time to change again.

When furnishing the nest, flee from any household salesman who claims that his goods will last a lifetime. She will want to buy them because they are more expensive than some other woman's, but regardless of their worth, they will show an astonishing degree of obsolescence within a year or two. It is cruelty to dumb animals to prevent a woman from refurnishing her home at least every five years; you are lucky if she does not insist that you rebuild the place as well. Buy cheap stuff that will look as run down as she describes it within that space of time. Throwing away cheap furniture is less of a struggle than parting with well made articles.

The first electric ice box we purchased lasted almost twenty years; the reason, I believe, was that the unit was shielded within a heavy steel ball. Otherwise I am sure my pride and joy would have stuck hairpins into the works in order to get rid of it. When I finally did agree to part with it, she could not be satisfied with any make but one which was famous for a complete breakdown within four or five years. We are back with the old make now, but they have learned their lesson and make no more lifetime refrigerators.

On the other hand, some women are a downright menace to progress. I remember about thirty-five years ago we bought a new washing machine. Because we had children who, like all kids, just loved to stick their fingers into the wringer, I coaxed my wife to try the new Savage.

This machine was the papa and mama of the modern washer, except it came only with a copper covered tub and when it was time to spin-dry the clothes one had to remove the top and lift one side of the basket until it would catch in a horizontal position. It worked fine until the other women got white enameled washers; then my pride and joy began to find fault with it. About this time one of our sons, who possessed an inquiring mind, put a cat into the basket and turned on the machine while it was in the spin-dry position. The results were hard on the cat and also on the boy's rear exposure. That was the clincher and we had to get rid of that machine.

We had several others, changing the washer when the laundry was redecorated for one of a harmonious color, and then came the automatics. The neighbor ladies all got them, so we had to spend three hundred dollars for the latest model. A couple of years ago, just after a mechanic had been out to patch up the works in the thing, my wife had a brainstorm and insisted that I turn it in and get her a washer with a wringer in which she could use all the soap she wanted and a lot less hot water. We got fifteen dollars for the automatic and she is as delighted with the "new" old-style machine as though it was a newly discovered scientific wonder. She swears her clothes are cleaner, she does much less work, and there is never any shortage of hot water.

When I think what would happen to this country if any sizeable portion of the female sex would revert to this type of decadent thinking, I shudder at the effect it would have upon our economy. Fortunately that type of woman is rare, and for the good of the business community should be locked up so that her treasonable conclusions not be broadcast. You, as a man, have an inborn reverence for old things and resist change with what little willpower the years of married life have left you, but it is a good thing for your job or business that your wife is not so constituted. Thanks to her, progress in America means bigger junk piles, faster and faster turnover in household furnishings.

You can be thankful that she expends her desire for the new and untried to furnishings and clothes and has not as yet adopted the Hollywood fashion of trading in the old husband for one who matches her current hair color more pleasingly.

Mechanization of our creative efforts is the thing that has destroyed man's loyalty to his company and his trade. The little boy who manufactures a toy wagon out of some scraps of lumber and old baby buggy wheels feels that he has accomplished something to be proud of. But how much pride does a man

The little boy has accomplished something to be proud of.

have in a big luxurious automobile when all that he has contributed to the task of manufacture is screwing certain nuts upon designated bolts? Of course he gets bored and gladly embraces the union doctrine that the manufacturer of the car or gadget is only a slave driver and that he himself is a most unhappy serf giving his life's blood that some man in the front office may live in a style to which *he* can aspire to only in his dreams.

Why has the home and the keeping thereof suddenly become so boring that all women wish to escape from it at the earliest opportunity? Simply because man's inventive genius has relieved her of all the tasks that made homekeeping worth-while.

Paying thirty-five cents for a loaf of bakery bread that comes already sliced and wrapped securely so it will remain fresh for days is a little thing and gives no sense of accomplishment. Compare this with the ritual of making yeast, and going through all the steps of producing a batch of home baked bread which contains only those ingredients known to be wholesome and healthful. Your wife's pleasure in watching the family consume the product of her labor should be reward in itself for her, somewhat like that which the mother robin experiences when she brings home a nice fat worm to her brood of hungry nestlings.

What satisfaction is there in popping a frozen dinner into the oven to heat? Did you ever hear of a lady inviting a marital prospect to come to dinner in her apartment, hoping to get him in a domestic mood, and then serving him a TV dinner and a cake manufactured by Betty Crocker, confessing that she had little hand in the preparation thereof? She may have served this ready-made fare, but she was careful to destroy the wrappings and accept his praises of her culinary art with maidenly modesty. She made sure he didn't learn that her only contribution to the feast was manipulating a can opener, and an electric one at that.

And her housekeeping is not always the way it looks in the living room on party nights. The fact is that a woman has a pack rat's temperament when it comes to collecting things which are of no earthly use to her or anybody else. I once purchased a house for investment and went back to look at it while the former owners were moving out. It was in good shape until I came to the room of a seventeen year old daughter. When her bed was moved out it revealed at least three wheelbarrows full of rubbish—dance programs, candy boxes, old shoes, discarded pennants, torn undergarments and hose, and everything else that would have awakened desire in a pack rat.

To the average man, nurses seem to be the most dedicated, neatest and most angelic of any women, and most of them are. But under that starched white uniform beats the heart of an average woman. In a small hospital we depend on a shifting population of nursing talent; they are truly wanderers, and when you hire one you have no idea whether she is a jewel or a joke. When one proves to be a reliable worker you pray that she will stay with you always. In fact most physicians who run small hospitals should practice polygamy and marry every good nurse that comes along to insure her remaining in his establishment. But look out for the dillies! I remember one wonderful nurse that dropped in from New York one time; we were sure we had a jewel. But after two weeks of service she left the ward where she was alone on duty without notifying anyone; three days later we got a telegram from her in Los Angeles where she was broke, in jail and getting over a big drunk. Another sister of mercy kept a little dog in her room, and when she left the hospital housekeeper found enough bones under her bed to feed a family of coyotes for a year. A third, the perfect picture of cleanliness and order, had a peculiar habit of wadding dirty diapers into a ball and dropping them into the linen closets instead of rinsing them out and putting them down the laundry chute. A fourth went out to a local dance one night, tried to steal another girl's boyfriend, and showed up at the hospital next morning with two black eyes. And yet, to see those ladies on the ward, one would suppose that a simple little fly or a loud word would throw them into hysterics.

I always liked to listen to other people tell about their troubles and when I was doing more traveling than I am today considered it rare fun to get the Pullman porters to raving about the ladies' rest rooms. I never saw the inside of any of them, but the descriptions were terrible.

Man himself is not the most orderly animal on earth, but he *will* burn his old socks and on occasion get a shovel and muck out the dump. His mate, however, has a decided prejudice against throwing away anything, except possibly his boots and fishing gear.

Women hate straight lines, the shortest distance between two points, and when at all possible will choose a more circuitous route in arriving at their mental destinations. I have always believed the common dollar sign ($) related more to matrimony than to money. We find the two straight vertical lines denoting the male pants-encased legs, while the female twines around them with the graceful curves of the letter S.

Following is a new approach to the old gag about buying a wife a brown purse and then having to buy her a whole new wardrobe to match the damned thing. About a year ago someone gave my wife a new kind of cracker jar guaranteed to keep crackers crisp and fresh; it was pink in color. Because the rest of her canisters and bread box were white, they had to go and were replaced by pink ones. Then we had to have a new kitchen table to contrast with all of this pink, so she bought a baby blue one, trimmed in copper. This made the floor covering look sort of beat-up, as it was mostly a darker blue, so a new linoleum was in order. This in turn made the walls look dull, so we painted them. Now the wall colors fight with the original pink cracker jar, so we have to replace the cracker jar, bread-box, etc., etc., with copper colored containers. That cracker jar will cost me five hundred dollars before I am at peace again.

To educate your wife in the proper conduct of financial affairs you must have the patience of Job, and insist that she go over your financial situation with you at every opportunity. It is a tough job, as I know from experience.

In my early married life I kept my safety deposit box in a large Salt Lake City bank. The safety deposit department was in the basement, and one entire wall was covered with a plate glass mirror about ten feet by twenty. We would go down there with the best of intentions, and for five minutes my wife would show interest in the contents of the box. However, if I happened to get too interested in what I was doing and ignored her for a minute, I would find her standing before that mirror, trying to see if her slip showed or if her stocking seams were in the true perpendicular.

As she grows older she takes more interest in monetary matters. She duly takes note of all dividends received and then forgets to put them in her account book, so every three or four months she has to borrow mine and copy her entries from it.

Regardless of the fact that she knows a lot of crooks call at every home and try to interest the wife in some haywire scheme, she will take the advice of any stranger in preference to my own. I am not saying that she isn't sometimes right in so doing; but after all, this marriage is a partnership and the junior member should defer to the senior occasionally, at least.

Stating it frankly, the true woman understands little and cares less about the business transactions of the family; she considers them to be the old man's job, just as preparing meals is hers. It takes a lot of patience to get her to understand or even be interested in balancing the checkbook, to say nothing of the income tax forms.

Every woman should have an allowance, both for her household expenses and for spending without any accounting. But you must watch this arrangement, as she enjoys money that she talks you out of much more than that which is her rightful share. All of our married life, before moving into a community property state, we maintained separate checking accounts in the bank. We went to Salt Lake City often, and just before we reached the city limits my wife would frantically search through her purse and discover that she had left her checkbook at home. Could she borrow ten or twenty dollars from me and pay it back when we returned? These little loans had to be classified as Permanent Investments.

Whether your little lady is interested or not, it is your husbandly duty to acquaint her with the ways of doing business and the rudiments of that most difficult art—hanging onto the money you do manage to accumulate. And she'll be contrary about that just as she is about everything else.

You can build her the most beautiful bathroom that either of you have ever seen, but you cannot force her to put the top back on the toothpaste tube or to resist the temptation to hang stockings over the shower curtain rod.

You can bellow and swear as loud and as long as you wish, but when she wants to rip a seam or sharpen a pencil the blade in your safety razor is the only tool in the house which will do a satisfactory job.

You may have learned to be neat and police up your side of the bedroom as if you were expecting an inspection tomorrow, but if you go over to her side in the dark you are going to step on half a dozen spike-heeled slippers.

If you drop an ash from your smoke on the living room rug you are promptly told about it, but five minutes later she sits down to read the paper or sew on a button and the place looks like a paper box factory after an explosion.

You can fill your wife's kitchen with labor-savers until it looks like the engine room of the *Queen Mary,* but you cannot prevent her from buying a doll-sized washboard and washing out a "few things" in the sink.

You can feed a cat cream and hummingbird's tongues until her sides stick out three inches, or you can beat her with a club until eight of her nine lives are gone, but you cannot break her of the habit of pouncing on birds. Beating up your wife does no more good than it does the cat, you might just as well do as the cattle on the range do in the winter when a northerner blows: turn your back to the storm and suffer it out.

If you want her to vote for some political party, pick out some good looking candidate on that ticket and begin to abuse him; swear that he beats his wife and steals pennies from the collection box in church. She will vote for him even if she knows nothing about his political complexion.

No defense attorney in his right mind would accept an all female jury for a woman client. If she was good-looking and dressed well such a jury would convict her on general principles, and if she wasn't the same verdict would be given.

Another thing you must accustom yourself to is the fact that your spouse is sure that she married the wrong man. If you are a physically perfect specimen of manhood, she wishes that she had passed you up and married a brain. And if you are a Ph.D. she wishes that she had married the captain of the football squad, even though he is now a truck driver.

No matter how well you feed a cat you will never break her of the habit of pouncing on birds.

If she has a suspicious lump in her breast she will cover it up and try to prevent her physician from discovering it, while if she is as healthy as a bear she is always running to a doctor to see if there isn't something wrong with her.

The one thing she *is* stable about is her obstetrician. If some old coot who never cleans his fingernails except on leap year calls the tune when she gives birth to her first-born and things go along all right, she will travel clear across the country and run all kinds of risks in order to get back to him when the second child is due.

She is strictly an individualist at heart and cares nothing about the rest of the world outside her own little family. I know this will bring screams of protest; there *are* women who seem to be great humanitarians, but they are the exception and are such because their lives are so dull they cannot stand them, or else they are women who have been thwarted in their natural functions and adopt the poor and downtrodden as substitutes for the families they never had. Compassion is not nearly so common among them as it is in men.

I have never done any research on the subject but I have heard that when women drown, the body floats upstream and the statement seems plausible.

An old Vermont granite cutter got depressed with life in general and women in particular several years ago, and wrote a country newspaper a letter about the situation. He said: "Man's life is full of crosses and temptations, and women are the cause of most of them. I came into this world without my consent, and I'll go out of it against my will. When I was little the big girls kissed me; now that I am big, the little girls kiss me. When I was poor my old lady said I was a bad manager; now that I am rich she says I am dishonest. When I went in for politics, she said it was for graft; now that I'm out of politics she says I'm no good to my country. If I give to charity it's for show; if I don't, I'm a stingy cuss. If I'm actively religious, I'm a hypocrite; when I take no interest in religion I'm a hardened sinner. If I show her any affection she thinks I'm a soft specimen; if I don't she howls about how cold-blooded I am. If I had died young, she would have thought there was a great future before me; since I've lived to an old age, she says I've missed my calling. I've finally got to admit that with women you can't win; you're damned if you do, and you're damned if you don't."

This poor fellow caught the essential element of all women —their eternal contrariness. It's a fact that they're the hardest creatures on the face of the earth to please. Girls are not contrary on purpose, they are simply constructed so that reason and logic seem to them the height of folly. Women's intuition is the only map by which they can travel. But the disgusting thing about the whole business is that they are more often right than you, with all of your research and fact finding.

In sailing the matrimonial bark, always point the ship in the direction you do not want to go.

8

Your Own Private Gettysburg

Gird me with strength for the battle.
PSALMS 18:39

THERE ARE A lot of similarities between the battle of the sexes and the cold war we have been enjoying with the Russians. Russia has adopted the female technique for keeping her adversary off balance down to the last comma, and Uncle Sam has shown a perfect picture of the bewildered male in his reactions.

The courtship went on during the last World War. Uncle Sam showered gifts upon this new-found partner, and received kind and gentle words of love from Russia, but she showed no disposition to bestow any gifts of love in return. The beautiful romance was pictured at Yalta by Russia, and our old Uncle lapped it up, despite the warnings of that elder brother England. At Potsdam the suitor fell for the age-old trick of deeding over half of his property to his ladylove before he got her name on the dotted line. Since that time it's been the usual course of married love, the wife blowing hot and cold by turns, and the husband totally confused by her changes of mood. Sometimes she is in the "how-dare-you" stage, a woman wronged. "How could you treat me so, you brute!" But when she wants to work this mixed-up husband for a new mink coat, along will come the forgiving smile and tears and once more he will awake in the morning nicely situated in the doghouse with his pockets picked again.

The similarity between our government's actions and that of its own male citizens goes even further. There was a time when this country was gloriously masculine, tending to its own business and insisting that other people do the same. But the depression of the thirties changed its character to such an extent that even our Creator must have developed grave doubts of its sanity.

The American male cast off his natural gift of being the architect of his own fortune, and with a mighty sigh of relief, placed dependence for his old age on the mighty shoulders of F.D.R. and got the Social Security Act. A man with a spark of initiative left in his soul was classed as an undesirable character and not allowed to work to support his family unless he would accept serfdom. All this is reflected in the individual citizen, his natural masculine nature is so tamed that his only desire is to get into a labor union that will do his thinking for him, or a company which supervises his every action, even the choice of his wife, all so that he may enjoy his social security, pension, sick insurance and all the other gimmicks classed under the broad skirts of the word *security.*

Such a fate would have been laughed out of court by his grandpa; all the security he wanted or got was what he secured for himself, and his only use for government was to have somebody to blame for his depredations on the Indians. Every time modern man accepts some government handout, he loses just so much of his masculine individuality. Thirty long years of father image, with the brief interlude when Harry tried unsuccessfully to instill some old Missouri stubborn mulishness into us, has just about plucked all the tail feathers from the American eagle and now the damned thing has begun to cluck.

Nature abhors a vacuum, and so woman has been filling up the space with her own untried personality. Now we are a matriarchal society, doomed to travel the paths of destiny tied to woman's apron strings until the time comes when some masculine horde overruns us and puts us out of our misery.

Now the damned thing has begun to cluck.

Why write a chapter about how to get along with women? One sentence is enough: Do as they tell you to do. Such a statement would have been ridiculous in our fathers' time; men got along with women by being supremely masculine, and women loved them for that attribute. Now that we have lost our sex characteristics women are not satisfied with either us or themselves in the driver's seat. If the rest of the world will just wait a decent interval, we will fall down in a heap of frustration and wipe ourselves from the map.

However, there are still ways in which a man can come out the victor in this momentous struggle, but he has to use female guile to accomplish the result. Instead of following our fathers' example of "You do this, *or else*," we must appear to give in to her every notion. Even though this entails a great loss of face, we have about reached the point where we haven't any face left to lose.

When some great problem comes up in your domestic relations, such as what color to paint the living room or the make of the new ice box, just think it through and then state your opinion; pay no attention to her arguments except to dodge the flying kitchen utensils and walk out when she begins to cry. Such tactics are worse than spying through the bathroom window, but the alternative is to spank her, and these athletic girls are hard to turn over your knee. So just state your opinions and shut up, delaying the call to the painter for a few days to let things develop. And they will.

She is unsure of her own opinion and only stuck up for it to humiliate you. Once you have withdrawn from the field of battle, doubts spring up in her knotty little head and within a week she returns to the attack, having stolen your arguments completely and just daring you to object to her logic. Don't ever mention that the idea originated with you in the first place, just yield gracefully and let her have her way. She knows that she has lost, but such action saves her face and she can pretend to be the victor.

I have found that this scheme works with women as patients, wives, and relatives in general. The only thing you have to do is to procrastinate in arriving at the point of action until the female has convinced herself that she thought your way all the time. Her supposed victory is sweet, and your own considered judgment prevailed. You will not lose face with her because deep down in her heart she knows you were the ultimate master of the situation, and with her perverse nature she wanted it that way all the time.

However, this technique is a tricky thing; you cannot make snap judgments and fly off the handle at the breakfast table. When the insults are flying thick and fast don't expect to come up with any commandments that would appear to have been handed to you on Mount Sinai. Disengage yourself from the battle and climb up your personal mountain for reflection and divine guidance before you present your decision; don't make the same mistake poor old Moses did by losing your head and cracking up your own commandments in her presence, even if she seems to be getting the best of the argument. It is just barely possible that she is right (not likely, of course, but possible), and in that case agree with her even if it gives you lockjaw to do so.

This technique is not a very honorable or masculine procedure, but remember that she, like the Russians, will use any trick or misrepresentation that comes into her brain to beat you. After all, if you win you got your way, which is a dear thing to a man. Maybe you cannot be a rat, but at least this makes you a long-tailed mouse, and such is better than being a louse!

There are certain fields in domestic relations that should be her responsibility, and others that are yours. Territories should be distinctly surveyed and boundary lines clearly drawn when you are bride and groom. As you expect her to keep her side working smoothly, so must you hoe your own row of corn. She has as much right to call attention to neglected weeds in the garden as you have to mention the dirty dishes in the sink. If you object to her appearance at breakfast, remember to shave on Saturday morning or expect a few remarks on the subject. If she married you under the impression that she was getting a man, for heaven's sake never let her discover that you are such a weak and spineless individual that you require frequent doses of alcohol to keep your masculinity showing.

Cocktails are a status symbol in our present society, but a man can accept one and fool with it all evening if he expects to drive home after the party. And a woman is justified in any measures short of murder in dealing with a drunken husband. And under certain circumstances I could almost condone *that* violent action. There is nothing that will so sour a doctor's compassion for the human race as to have some drunk brought into the emergency room full of booze and smelly foods and have him unchuck the mess all over the clean floor in the middle of the night when nurses are scarce and he has to clean up the mess himself.

I remember one such incident when a tunnel superintendent came in with a lacerated scalp caused by his wife beaning him with a jack handle after he had blackened her eye on the road home from a party. I shaved his scalp with a dull razor and sewed up the laceration with as large a needle as I could find and forgot the anesthetic. It gained me the nickname of "Old Rough Jesus" among his contemporaries, but in the future most of the drunken brawlers went to other doctors to be repaired.

Just remember this the next time you decide to fly your kite: only men suffering from a feeling of inferiority require a cargo of alcohol to make them feel equal to their fellows. If you are a man who has any pride in yourself, you can have just as good a time on one cocktail as on ten, and you don't look nearly so ridiculous to other people. There is nothing so pitiful and disgusting as a man, the image of his Maker, acting like a hog that has been fed fermented grain (and that goes for women too, doubled and redoubled).

Like all things that go to make human existence less than divine, domestic brawling is not a unique aspect of the present generation. There were just as many Xanthippes in grandpa's day as there are at present, but they were a little more restrained in bringing their troubles into the divorce courts. Even in that glorious past women took offense at things that seemed trifling compared to the importance they tried to attach to the transgression.

One such incident occurred in my intern days when I was not as experienced in the ways of a woman's heart and mind as I was to become in later years. A young female patient was brought to the hospital in a paddy wagon. The cop told me that she had killed her lover and winged his current girlfriend in a bar and then tried to shoot herself. A guard was placed at the door of her room and I was supposed to care for her and get her back to health so that she could be tried for murder.

I was much interested in this case because, like most of my male contemporaries, I had occasionally been guilty of trying to love more than one girl at a time, never dreaming that such serious consequences might occur. I felt that I had better find out the history of this affair so I could avoid such embarrassing events in my own love life.

She was most willing to talk and I got the following sad tale, which went to prove that the poet was right when he said "Hell hath no fury like a woman scorned." She had loved this man and turned most of her earnings in the practice of the oldest profession over to him, that he might live in ease and comparative luxury. Then she caught him in this night club spending her earnings on another woman. She stated that she had loved the guy with all her heart, so much so that she would even have gone homesteading with him, had he asked her to make this supreme sacrifice. If she could not have him no blanked-blanked other girl could either, so she shot him, and only regretted that her aim had been at fault when she trained her artillery upon the other woman. Now that he was dead she didn't want to live, and would I please fix her wounds so they would be fatal, which unfortunately was impossible.

I was new to the West at the time and did not appreciate the depth of her affection for the trifling brute, but once I become acquainted with homesteaders and their wives out in the great American desert I realized that "A greater love hath no man than this." A dame who would willingly hole up in a jerry built shack, twenty miles from water, forty from a tree, and perhaps a hundred from any other human being except her whiskery and dirty husband, her only neighbors smelly sheep, rattlesnakes and coyotes, such a woman must be consumed by a love "that passeth all understanding."

A greater love hath no man than this.

Everything a man learns can be of use to him sometime; when the time came for me to test a woman's love I invited the girl to set up housekeeping with me in a situation which boasted all of the above listed handicaps except lack of neighbors, and she was nuts enough to do it. It is a good idea to show the girl all the disadvantages of so-called wedded bliss before you ask for her decision. If she doesn't love you enough to go homesteading with you, she had better be passed up; there are times in any married relationship when homesteading would be the lesser evil.

There are other tricks of the trade that a husband can play. Remember the little lady never gets tired of anything that she thinks some other woman might want, and if you would be a happy husband you should take advantage of this weakness.

There are some strange things written in the Bible which, quoted out of context, make fine reading. I direct your attention to I Thessalonians, Chapter 5, verse 22: "Abstain from all appearance of evil." Many a man has tried to follow that injunction literally and got caught at it, so I would advise you to avoid evil, but under certain circumstances do not try too hard to avoid the *appearance* of same. If you can live an upright life and still make your wife believe that you are a bit susceptible to other women's charms and that they are interested in charming you, you will be less likely to end up with a wife who is bored by married life.

Just why this is, I do not know, nor does any other man. When we get married we want the woman to be ours alone, we resent any show of interest in another man, and react like mad bulls if anyone shows an interest in her. But it is terribly boring to a woman to be the possessor of a male that arouses no envy in another woman's breast.

I had that lesson brought home to me most forcibly very early in my young manhood. I was working as a telegrapher in a small station down in Missouri. The agent in charge of the station was having domestic troubles because his wife insisted upon taking the children and making long visits at her parents' home, leaving him to batch for a good part of the time. Like all men, he hated this chore, and finally decided to use a slightly underhanded method of keeping the little woman at home.

One day when I was going to the nearest large town he asked me to purchase a type of comb the girls were wearing at the time to retain what they called "rats" in the hair. These combs were shaped like a half circle which fit over the top of the head, and they were often quite fancy with brilliants.

I took a girl along to be sure I purchased the proper article. When I returned and gave my friend the merchandise he astonished me by breaking it in the middle and discarding half of it in the waste basket. He refused to state how he was going to use the other piece, and advised me to wait and watch developments. Pretty soon his wife returned from a visit and like all wives at once proceeded to clean up the mess—changing the beds, etc., etc., etc. Before the day was out she came charging down to the depot like a hog going to war, with this half comb clutched in her hot little hand. She gave him the devil, right in front of me, accusing him of everything in the book. She had found the comb under his bed, right where he had placed it, and circumstantial evidence was enough to convict him of gross infidelity in her eyes. I worked there for six months after that storm, and she never left home for an overnight stay in all that time.

That was one way in which a slight appearance of evil served a good purpose, and I have seen many a home whose martial and marital relations would have been improved by some such strategy. Some wives seem determined to dominate the household and use every trick in the book to make hubby lose face, and unfortunately many of them succeed. A man who loses face at home is bound to reflect his inferior position by his actions, and soon other men on the job begin to treat him with as little consideration as he receives off the job. Even in my day many good men were ruined by this handicap, and now that women are working outside the home and at times bringing in more money than their mates, the condition is becoming more prevalent and as a result there are more divorces and broken homes.

Remember, she may fight you like a tiger to impose her will upon you, but she hopes that you will slap her down either literally or figuratively and will be even more upset if you fail to do so. Don't apply brute force unless you are big enough to take her over your knee and spank her; a black eye may be used as evidence in court, but no woman will expose a reddened bottom to the jury.

Of course, like Shakespeare I would teach twenty but fail to follow my own teaching. I have never found it necessary to adopt such violent measures in my own family, but I have seen a lot of wives just spoiling for a spanking. A man must be a leader in his home if he expects to make progress in his activities away from home. The Orientals are not the only people to whom the loss of face is a calamity. Be a leader and not a driver in your domestic relations and remember this one fact: Every woman yearns to play the lead all the time, and when she seems to have lost her marbles just try and understand that she is playing the heroine in some self-constructed drama. If it doesn't strain your self-control too much go along with the act and play the part of the villain just for kicks.

If she seems to be falling down in the part she will be sure to revert to the roles made so popular by the divine Sarah Bernhardt, drop over on the floor and appear to be breathing her last. This is the time to call in the neighbor ladies who will appreciate her efforts and join in the act, rushing around with hot towels, cold towels, smelling salts and what-have-you. Somebody will insist that you call the doctor. If the doc is wise in the ways of women, he will banish all the others, tell her to get up off the floor, and demand to know what the row was about in the first place. And will she tell him. But don't worry— he is a man too, and won't believe a tenth part of it.

When you first put a halter on a baby calf and try to teach him to lead, he will buck, plunge, and try to tangle your legs up in the rope; but once he finds that you stand firm he trots along beside you and seems to enjoy the performance. Leading a family is much the same process, first the wife and then each kid in turn must understand that papa is the ultimate authority. You can spoil a calf by kicking his ribs, but improve his performance by a light switch applied to his tail region, and so is it the way with the human family. Be firm, and if necessary switch them a little, but never lose your temper in the process.

Getting along with women is sometimes a greater problem

than the State Department ever had to meet. As man becomes more of a conformist and allows his government to do his thinking for him, he definitely loses face with that greatest of non-conformists, his wife, and the battle becomes more equal than the one his father had to fight. Love conquers all, but like the nations Uncle Sam has conquered in the past, somehow love's conquests do not always stay conquered. We, as a nation or as individual males, can no longer expect to occupy the exalted position to which we once were accustomed and must share our eminence on the dung heap with these other forces. Will we be able to work out a satisfactory code of Peaceful Co-existence with them?

Not being a diplomat, I will refrain from sketching out a plan on a world wide scale. I have, however, lived in close association with the women of our country for some seventy-five years, and am most proud to state that I have never been shot at and am in no immediate danger of bombing from that quarter. Once this book is published this personal and peaceful co-existence may end abruptly should any women happen to read it and rightly consider it a provocative gas attack, but we will not endeavor to look into the future.

There are certain rules which, if followed with reasonable compliance, will I am sure promote a degree of domestic peaceful co-existence and that is the best we can hope for in marriage relationships. My wife and I have followed them for nearly half a century without actually taking up arms against each other, and so I recommend them to you.

1. The first and most important: pick a wife who is the exact opposite of what you know your own personality to be.

    If you like to talk, pick one who prefers listening; if you are the silent type, pick one of the southern belles whose tongue is anchored in the middle and who can talk about her relations all day without stopping for refreshments. (Being a bit hard of hearing yourself is a distinct advantage.)

    If you get mad quickly and blow up like a sky rocket

at the least provocation, pick one that is a slow starter; that kind burns longer, but you can escape before she takes off.

2. Sign the following pre-marital agreement: The inside of the house is hers, with the exception of your closet and the region around your favorite chair. In turn assign her a flower bed for her very own in the garden and never so much as pull a weed therefrom or offer a suggestion that she might improve its appearance by so doing.

3. Agree that any expenditure of over twenty-five dollars be a joint project, only to be consummated after a calm and deliberate debate.

4. Limit the family's indebtedness to what can be liquidated easily within one year on your present income, with the possible exception of a home.

5. Promise that you each will refrain from spying on each other, but if the other's actions are not understood, ask for an explanation at once.

6. Agree that the only valid reason for either one of you denying the other sexual satisfaction is being laid up in the hospital in a knee-to-neck body cast. (By rights, if the little lady isn't in the mood for endless weeks you should be free to go elsewhere, but God help you if you try it. And if you'd rather watch the late-late show than play with her, you're the one that's falling down on the job.)

7. Stipulate that no female relatives of either party will be allowed to visit in your home for more than a combined total of three days each year.

8. Agree that at parties and in bars one of you will stay on the wagon, the better to drive it home. Better yet, both of you stay sane so you'll still be talking the same language at the end of the evening. When in doubt, budget for that long hack ride.

9. Agree that when children come neither partner will

ever countermand an order given them by the other, and for the children's sake that you will appear to be the head of the house and your wife will appear to defer to you when in their presence, and never have a real battle in front of them. (Kids are little savages and cannot understand peaceful co-existence.)

If your pride and joy absolutely demands violent action in a release from the dull existence I have described above, do not try to injure her except in her pride. A woman is only exceeded by the cat in her distaste for being the butt of laughter. If you are sure you can, spank her, otherwise think up some silly stunt.

The best one I ever heard of occurred in one of my patient's families. The wife was one of the black-haired fire-brands, and at times required forceful action to keep her ego in working order. One hot July day she had spent the entire morning at the beauty parlor sitting under the hair dryer and having a beautiful job of curls constructed; she was to be co-hostess at a dinner party that evening. At lunch she objected to something her husband said and threw her knife across the table at him. He retaliated by picking up a large bowl of gooey salad dressing and neatly upending it on the top of her shiny new hairdo, and then walked out laughing. She didn't kill him only because she couldn't catch him, and he, the unfeeling wretch, went downtown and told the whole story to his cronies. It would have taken a woman of stronger moral fiber than she to have faced the community after that episode; that night she left town and never came back.

So my advice to you is: Play the Lord and Master only when you are sure you can get away with it. Quit trying to gain your objectives in the bull-like manner that is part of your nature. Learn the female tricks of evasion, compromise and camouflage —"If you can't lick 'em, join 'em!" You have traded your birthright for a mess of security pottage, your tail feathers now resemble a flag of surrender rather than the bright badge of courage, and it behooves you to establish your real masculine dominance firmly before trying to wield it roughly.

If you remember to act like a MAN at all times instead of like a spoiled brat, your wife will cause you more joy and fulfillment than any other association on earth. At times the wind will blow cold, and when it does remember to follow the example of the cattle on the range: turn your backside to the blast and wait it out; the sun will shine again and be more beautiful for the darkness that preceded its coming.

And may the Lord bless thee and keep thee and give thee peace.

9

"Dear, I've Got Something to Tell You"

My dear angel has been qualmish of late, and begins to grow remarkably round in the waist.
TOBIAS SMOLLET

BY PROVING THAT the girls are not a part of the human race we have got ourselves out on a limb and sawed it off. Male ethical principles are a poor rule by which to measure female behavior. We do not expect a cat to act like a dog, to think like a dog, or to accept discipline like a dog. Neither can we hope that the female will accept man's standards and obey his laws, except as they coincide with her own desires and standards of deportment.

To understand her viewpoint we must go back to the savage and begin our research at that point. In that state women, along with other female animals, had but one driving impulse: the bearing of offspring and caring for them during the period of their dependency. The adult male was of no more importance than a buck deer, and was only allowed in the herd at times of heat or rut. His duty was to initiate the cycle of life renewing itself, but his interest in the matter was short-lived and he couldn't have cared less about subsequent events.

In the purely biological sense, one man could accommodate

twenty females. Like the lower animals, he got his greatest thrill in killing off his brothers; the more of them he eliminated, the more women he could serve. Wars were waged so that the surplus males might be disposed of. This led to a development which still curses us and accomplishes only one purpose: during, and for a few years after a war the female becomes more productive and clutters up the world with even more potential cannon fodder.

Man could not fight constantly, and so he was left with a lot of time on his hands. He began to think, as the simple result of plain boredom. He evolved a lot of ethical principles and tried to force them upon his neighbors, reserving the right to set them aside when the occasion seemed to warrant doing so. To show his superiority of mind he tried to unravel the secrets of the universe.

Now pregnancy is a time consuming affair and the rearing of children even more so. The female was pretty well occupied as long as her body was fruitful. One of her greatest problems today is to hold the breeding instinct in check and be faithful to the poor dope she married.

As we continue our study of the female we must not forget that this little instinct is at the bottom of her apparent lack of stability in character and action. If modern woman was allowed the privilege of mating with her choice of males, ninety per cent of us old guys would be bachelors. Woman has partially suppressed her desire for a perfect mate for the sake of the security of having some lesser male accept the responsibility of caring for her and assisting in the raising of her brood. She considers that she has paid a high price for security and feels little if any twinges of conscience if she occasionally gives way to this primal mating instinct. Monogamy is not a natural state with *either* sex, but in the male its nonobservance is simply a form of indoor sport, while his partner looks beyond the moment of ecstasy and fixes her mind's eye upon the results of the union.

As we proceed with this study we must never forget that man's mind and efforts are centered upon his immediate environment and the improvement thereof. He tries to accomplish his desires with as little physical effort as possible. His mate, meanwhile, is looking beyond the distant mountains to the bringing forth of offspring that may scale the heights. Man and wife are two people united in the bonds of holy matrimony, but with different goals and divergent viewpoints. The laws of the state and the church were made by men; if women decide to circumnavigate them, who are we to judge their actions?

There are three kinds of women: those who want babies and know it, those who want babies and *don't* know it, and those who should never have been mothers anyhow. The child is most fortunate if he draws the type of mother who welcomes him, because this type of woman will do anything and suffer any hardship to fulfill her maternal desires.

There are women who should never have been mothers.

One time I had a woman patient who earnestly desired a child and did not seem to be able to conceive. She lived with her longing for several years and then the husband got into trouble by fathering a child of another woman. She heard about it and was terribly upset. The child was up for adoption, and like a fool I suggested to the woman that here was her chance to become a mother of a child who needed one badly, and though it wasn't hers, at least it could claim relationship to the other side of the house. She was horrified at the thought, but I got the baby and took it over for her to look at, and finally she consented. Three years later, when this little girl was developing into a jewel of a child, the mother returned to my office and asked if I knew the whereabouts of the real mother. I did not, but asked her why. She blushed crimson and replied, "I was thinking about sending my husband back there and getting a little brother or sister for my baby, as I don't believe children should be raised all alone." Greater love hath no woman than that.

When we look back at the hazards the babies of thirty years ago had to avoid or suffer the consequences, we see that it must have been the work of an all-seeing power, toughening them up for the even greater hazards of their adult years. Babies pulling pans of hot water and grease from the stove and covering themselves with burning fluid was commonplace. Falling out of the back seat of moving automobiles was equally common, but the most unnecessary and painful way to cripple the kids was to go out to hang up the clothes and leave the wringer turning. For years we found it necessary for a doctor to be available at the office from eight to twelve o'clock every Monday morning because we knew that it would be a rare Monday that some poor little kid didn't show up with a mangled hand and forearm that he had tried to push through the wringer on the washing machine. They recovered nicely as a rule because a baby's ability to grow new skin and muscles is so much greater than an adult's. But it seemed that the mothers just didn't give a hoot what became of their infants; small loss and easily replaced, I guess. I realize that is an exaggeration, but sometimes it seemed true.

Nature does funny things sometimes just to confound us doctors. I once saw a girl baby that sat down in her bath before the mother had added any cool water to the boiling contents of the teakettle that had just been poured into the basin. She was parboiled all over her delicate region. After dressing her the best I could, I gave detailed instructions about sanitary care and showed the mother just how to handle the situation. They lived some forty miles out on the desert and there was no professional help in that region. In ten days they brought the patient in and with her all the dressings I had given them, intact in their original wrappings. They had not removed her diaper for the whole ten days because she cried when they attempted to do so. Once we got the filth peeled off I never saw a more beautiful result. The skin had recovered beautifully; what had looked like a piece of raw meat now resembled the two halves of a nicely ripened peach.

Some people's kids never got hurt at home, and others were always in the doctor's office. I remember one little chap who broke one arm one day and the other one the next; was he a power in the neighborhood for a time, a plaster club on each arm. Somehow it always seemed to be about one family in ten that had all the accidents, and they were usually the same people whose houses burned down and whose cars got wrecked. The parents seemed to try as hard as other people, but somehow they were always asking for an accident to happen.

This was the evidence that convinced me that some women were never meant to be mothers in the first place. In fact, real mothers are about as scarce as real wives, and the pattern begins to show within a month after they become pregnant.

Some woman may feel like adding a note here stating that real mothers occur more frequently than real fathers, and I would have to agree with them. But this book is about women, and after all they are the main architects of the family and of much more importance in erecting a pleasant and safe environment for the young than the fathers.

The child reflects his mother's influence in at least seventy-five per cent of his adult personality. A good woman can raise a nice bunch of kids with a drunken lout for a father who contributes nothing to his offspring except a microscopic little pollywog to fertilize the egg. A good man with a drunken shiftless wife just cannot overcome her influence and the kids usually would be better off drowned at birth. Worthless husbands have been the saving grace that made a lot of women wonderful mothers; that fierce loyalty of a female to her offspring has made saints out of a lot of otherwise pretty common female clay, even though the woman wasn't enthusiastic to begin with.

One illustration will be sufficient; a young woman had married an old bachelor who seemed to have plenty of money. Neither of them desired children so of course she got pregnant within a month. She was fit to be tied, and raised all kinds of hell. Finally, in desperation, the cause of it all called me to come and see her. She was putting on quite a show and when I arrived, playing Little Eva, you could almost see the lily in her hand and hear the rustle of the angels' wings. I was a bit grouchy myself that morning, so I listened to her tale of woe in silence and quickly started to leave. Her worried protector followed me to the door.

"Well, as long as you say she is not dangerously ill, I suppose I'll just have to humor her as best I can until she gets used to the new situation," he said. His back was to the stairway, but I could see his wife peeping over the bannisters above.

"Humor her, hell!" I replied. "She would recover quicker if you took her over your knee and lammed the daylights out of her."

This brought a snort from above and she yelled, "Him and who else? The two of you couldn't spank me."

I threw down my hat and bag and started up the stairs two at a time. "Do you want to bet?" She retreated to her bedroom and locked the door, yelling through the crack, "You're a damned old savage and I'll never speak to you again."

How did it turn out? Just like they always do; within a week she was down at the office with her little bottle for examination, as mild as a dish of rice pudding. Nature smiled upon her, presented her with a nice baby girl and turned her into a wonderful mother.

A doctor gets pretty well acquainted with his patient during the period of gestation, particularly if he is interested in the patient rather than his fee. I was egotistical enough to think I could foretell the type of mother a woman would make long before she was put to the test. I made some mistakes, but I was more often right than wrong. The girl who came into the office not necessarily overjoyed at the prospect of becoming a mother, but who accepted the added responsibility without complaint, who never uttered a disparaging word about her husband, who accepted my instructions without protest and tried her best to carry them out, was most likely to develop into a kind and understanding mother who would raise her kids with respect for law, order and their male parent.

On the other hand, the intensely feminine, selfish little brute who knocked her husband and tried to flirt with the doctor just from force of habit, who gave way to her appetite and added pounds of blubber for her already overworked body to contend with, and who then tried to blame either her husband or doctor for her transgressions, was the type of woman who would bring up her children to be selfish, without respect for their male parent, willing victims to any temptation that might come along. These girls subconsciously hated the child within them because its growth spoiled their pride and joy, their intensely feminine shape and allure for men in general. They were more interested in how their breasts would look after the ordeal was over than the appearance of the baby.

Believe it or not this worry also affected the husbands who were to become fathers for the first time. I well remember one grateful papa who was waiting for me to arrive at the office the day after his baby was born with a roll of bills clutched in his little hot hand. I told him my fee and he quickly placed the money on my desk remarking, "Gosh, Doc, it's worth ten times that much to have her looking like a human being again." And that is as it should be: a mother's first question—"Is my baby all right?" and the father's—"Is my wife going to be okay again?"

The new father will learn to love that baby or to resent it, according to the attitude of the mother. If she regards it as *her* baby, he will never care for it as much as the man whose wife regards the new arrival as *our* baby, and who treats him as though he were the only man on earth who could have initiated such a miracle. That is the family for which the doctor will try to do the impossible. When misfortune strikes them regardless of his efforts, it leaves him in a black mood, tempted to throw his medical equipment into the river and get a job sheep-herding.

Sometimes we get a queer mixture in the prospective mother. I remember one young bride who was so overcome with the prospect of motherhood that she sneaked off to the city and sought the services of an abortionist. After she had found him she came back to me and was a very sick woman for weeks. Six months later she became pregnant again, was as happy as a lark and developed into a wonderful mother and wife. But that case was unusual; most of the selfish little vixens carry on in the path they start with.

With some women the whole period of gestation is one long battle with the doctor, and I have often advised them to pack up their doll rags and hunt another doctor, and the contrary little devils wouldn't even do that.

This period can also be a battle between husband and wife about the expense of having a baby. Doctor bills, bills for maternity garments, bills for fitting up the spare room for a nursery because precious must have his own room and bath. You may mention having read that hospitals found out that babies did better when their crib was close to mother's bed, but don't mention it; Marge's pediatrician told her to fit up a complete suite for her baby, so she must do likewise. Think of the pleasure she will get in dolling this baby's bower up in frilly pink things, and her tears of disappointment and extra decorating bills if the kid happens to come equipped with testicles. Why these innocent little organs are so allergic to pink, no man will ever know.

The babe is born and you get the bill from the obstetrician and the hospital and if you don't go down to the bridge and jump in the river in despair you are a brave though discouraged young man.

You will hear a lot of arguments about how nice it is for the husband to be with his wife when the child is born, how it gives them a "togetherness" feeling that nothing else can do. I've seen a lot of men shanghaied into these performances and there was definitely no feeling of togetherness evident in the atmosphere. First she is having to work like the devil and she knows just whose fault it is, or pretends to know. She is a re- markable woman if she doesn't discuss your ancestors in a somewhat derogatory manner, and your own feelings are most likely centered upon your digestive tract.

Having babies is a messy business. When confronted by such the male is inclined to toss his hash, and that takes all of the togetherness out of the affair as far as he is concerned. Women are in no way affected by the sight of blood, but a man who does not instinctively shudder at it is slightly inclined toward sadism. He may get used to it but he never enjoys it. Most doc- tors wear rubber gloves not only to protect both themselves and the patient from cross infection but also because they hate to touch the stuff. Stay out of the delivery room and let your sex be represented by the poor sap who chose obstetrics for his profession.

When the big day arrives most women appear at the hospital with all the frilly clothes they possess and during delivery vent their spleen upon the poor embarrassed papa-to-be and insist upon being put to sleep at once and having forceps used to deliver the baby. When this is refused, they include the doctor in the brute classification along with their husbands, and once back in their beds spend their time trying to find things to com- plain about.

I remember one such dame who drove the nurses and dieti- cian about crazy with her whims, so they decided to serve her a banquet—double portions of everything including flowers on her tray. When it was served the housekeeper went along and asked her if there was anything else the lady could wish. The mother looked over the cargo of food and smiled in a sick kitten manner and said, "Well, I usually have two teabags in my cup at home."

Once these women are on their feet they are willing for any- body to take charge of the baby; even the mother-in-law is acceptable. They neglect the child as much as they can and spend the time squalling to the doctor because of the slight scar upon the abdomen where the muscles were stretched during gestation. When anybody is around and justifies the designation of "captive audience," they recite the grim details of the birth process in full, making it sound like all the horrors they ever saw on the midnight show at the movie house on Hallowe'en. They wind up the discourse with that old familiar line, "Why, the doctor told us that it was the most difficult birth he ever witnessed, and that I was the bravest little woman on earth to undergo such torture just to save my baby from harm."

When the kid needs his pants changed, it is anybody's baby, but before an audience it is always *her* baby, in spades. As the child grows older she farms him out on anybody she can get and insists that her husband take her to every get-together within a hundred miles. Should the brat get sick or hurt she rushes home with ribbons flying, screaming for her darling baby and gathering him to her breast like the shepherd in the old song about the ninety and nine lambs and the one that was lost. Like as not the kid doesn't recognize her and cries all the harder to get back to the current foster mother.

It would be a natural assumption that since women were intended by nature to have the children there would also have been some instinct given them about raising the offspring. Birds, cows, and guinea-pigs seem to know what to do once the little ones arrive, and in the dark and dismal past woman must have been gifted with this ability or the race would have died out ages ago.

Civilization has done queer things to us; in order that we might have indoor plumbing and washing machines we have sacrificed our natural keenness of scent, eyesight, and hearing, as well as our ability to judge the nourishing attributes of a food by the taste thereof. Woman as a product of this evolutionary change has lost in a great measure her ability to think and act the part of the mother, and but for Dr. Spock the babies of this country would be in a bad way.

Just why women insist that they are gifted with the foresight and wisdom necessary to run the country, and yet depend upon some man to tell them how to raise their babies, a primal obligation of their sex, is one of the paradoxes that cause man to think them slightly batty. It would seem that the spectacle of man trying to improve upon nature and making a holy mess of things in general would be a warning to them. Yet though they are much closer to the savage in their makeup, still they look to bungling man to guide them in their most important mission in life. A man's advice about raising the children must of necessity come from knowledge gained only by observation and not by doing the actual experiment. And yet woman, the creator of life, entrusted by the Creator with the nourishment of the same, will deny the child his birthright and stuff him full of some compound of synthetic ingredients. Salesmen of drug manufacturing firms have convinced doctors that these synthetics will nourish the babies better than mother's milk, or at least guarantee fewer upsets of colic in the middle of the night, a consummation to be wished for by all men of the healing arts.

During my years of medical practice I was the all-wise guide for the feeding and care of perhaps two thousand children. When I became a farmer I tried to raise something over a dozen baby calves by scientific methods, and each and every one of the calves suffered from the bellyache until I finally got disgusted and turned them out with their mothers, with happy results for all concerned. Just what does that prove? Simply that human babies are more resistant to insults and made of sterner stuff than are the members of the bovine family. But is that any reason why we should insult babies' digestive tracts with a mixture of half-ripe pears and raw liver rather than the food nature took ages to perfect?

It was never intended that males, physicians or not, should govern the raising of infants any more than that of roosters or bulls. Unlike cows and hens, women have pawned that chore off on the awkward sex that they themselves might have more time to pursue that false search for their own personalities.

Whenever I happen to be on a bus, train, or plane and see some young mother grab a can opener and a spoon and a can of some mixture and begin shoveling the cold and nasty looking goop into her tiny offspring, I am reminded of the wisdom of those children of nature, the Goshute Indian squaws of my early practice. These ladies traded the cans of baby food I gave them to the saloon keeper for a liquid of proven potency which they promptly drank, and let the kids get along the best they could with nature's brew. Their babies thrived upon this natural elixir of mother's milk fortified by a bit of the panther secretion plus perhaps the addition of an occasional supplementary feeding of ground-squirrel soup seasoned with black ants. I never saw a case of convulsions from digestive troubles among the Indian babies, but I have seen plenty among the whites who were experimenting with new and highly recommended and advertised patent baby foods.

The white mother's reactions to this not uncommon emergency in the life of her baby was always a puzzle to me; at the first sign of something seriously wrong she flung the baby onto the bed and rushed out of the house yelling, "My baby! Oh, my baby!" Some neighbor usually called the doctor.

One of the favorite stunts the loving mothers employed to cheer up the doctor's weary and monotonous day was to leave salted peanuts around where the toddlers could reach them. A bunch of half-chewed peanuts can produce some astonishing results in the infant's stomach and cause more intense excitement and entertainment for the ladies of the neighborhood than the appearance of a rattlesnake crawling in the front door.

As the child progresses out of the infant stage, women inflict more indignities upon him. If he is a boy he may have to wear long curls until he is ten years old, and is brought up to consider his dad a few cuts worse than Simon Legree in *Uncle Tom's Cabin*. Naturally he develops into a little snob, despised by the other kids on the block and the cause of his dad forever wearing that shamed-faced apologetic air of a man who must cringe whenever sons are mentioned in masculine company.

After the child has driven numerous well-trained teachers of the school, music and dancing variety out of their chosen professions into matrimony or attempted homicide, he is sent off to a school where his wonderful talent will be appreciated. And if somebody doesn't drown him before he reaches man's estate, he marries some innocent female and condemns her to a life of frustration. His mother is always there to see that the wife does right by "my darling boy."

If the old mother-in-law can cause a breakup in the marriage she feels as happy as a hen that laid a golden egg, and weeps and wails about the way the world is treating her offspring. Her other kids? She never had any; papa never again had his opportunity to play that joke upon her and probably never wanted to anyway. She had everything she could buy on credit and did her best to make other women dissatisfied with their husbands, and flirted with all the males she met until old age pulled the string. Her husband, of course, developed into the sort of a man that would ask her permission to put on his Sunday britches. Soft as a newborn kitten and as hard as battleship steel, she is a product no metallurgist ever even dreamed of making, but the world is full of them.

I once had the opportunity to vent my spleen on one of these pussycats, and it was sweeter than getting a book on the best seller list. It was a quadrangle instead of the usual three-sided affair, and our heroine was away on a visit. Due to a mixup in the signals, both the other husband and wife showed up only minutes apart at the home where only the husband was present. The other wife, being an aggressive type, took the offensive and called the turn upon her erring mate before he had time to ask why she was visiting her neighbor at such an hour. In the ensuing passage at arms she hit him over the head with a vase and I got in on the repair work. I got most of the story from their remarks, as the battle was not yet over.

When the heroine came home her heartsick man broke down and told how he had been stepping out on her, and she promptly had hysterics. Again I was called and found her lying stretched out on the bed. I sent the hubby out to my car for my bag, stating that I would have to give her a hypo. While he was gone I told her what I had learned at the other house and added that if she didn't cut out her monkey shines I would spill the whole story when hubby got back. I knew that she would gladly have killed me, but that there were no weapons handy, so I poured it on, just getting even with her and all of her ilk that had caused me so much trouble over the years.

Hubby returned and she greeted him with a smile that would have melted butter, had him kneel at the side of her bed and informed him, "Dear Dr. Peck has shown me that I have been neglecting you and that it was my fault that you forgot your marriage vows, so I will forgive you and try and be a more thoughtful wife in the future." He began to bawl and tried to take her in his arms, but she resisted saying, "Remember dear, my weak heart." When I cleared my throat as though to speak, she said, "Well maybe it won't hurt me to let you hold me this once."

Somehow it seems that I enjoyed that night call more than any other that I ever made, even though I was never called to administer to that family again.

When I think of my own sinful life, I wonder if I should tell her story even now because I will probably see her nicely situated with a pot of pitch in each hand waiting to welcome me in the sweet bye and bye. That type of woman seems to be the kind that takes hold of the imaginations of historians and novelists because she attracts men so easily, and consequently has given the sex a poor rating over the ages.

There is a kind of panic that comes to maternal women during their thirties which is not understandable to their husbands; it is the terror at the prospect of an empty nest. If your little family is growing out of the baby age and depending less and less upon the mother, you will see that she has less to do and the future without the familiar patter of little feet seems bleak indeed. You have been counting the cost (and realizing that each baby will set you back somewhere between twenty-five and fifty thousand dollars of your hard-earned money before it is ready to fly out from under your wing), are ready to call it quits. Here you have got to watch your step.

I remember one time an irate husband entered my office and made a few remarks, the tone of which was that as a diagnostician I was probably a good plumber. Among other things he mentioned was the fact that I had examined his wife a few weeks before and made a serious mistake in my findings. I was pretty sure that I had not seen his wife in months, but knowing women I thought it best to withhold the information and see what happened. (Women were forever quoting the doctor to prove a point and neglecting to inform the doctor about their using him as an argument to confirm their acts or conclusions.

If you told the husband that his wife was a liar, you made an enemy of both of them, while if you passed it off she would not forget your kindness and he would soon forget all about it.)

They were both nearing forty and had three well grown children when something happened.

The next day the man returned full of humility and apologies; it seemed that she wanted a baby, they were both nearing forty and had a grown family of three and he felt that he had his work cut out for him in giving the other children an education, so denied her pleadings. One day she came home from a shopping trip and informed him that the old doc had examined her and told her that her fertile period was past and that she could not hope to be a mother ever again. So the old man got careless with the inevitable result. She got her baby—and I got paid for delivering it.

When I think of the hundreds of gentle ladies who placed themselves under my care in their time of gestation and birth, accepted their role without complaint, worked like soldiers that their babies might come into the world as healthy as possible, who cared for those kids as best they could and put up with an erring husband more often than not, I am ashamed to sully their portraits with such she-devils as I have just been describing. But it takes all kinds of people to make a world. How anybody can live nine months with a stranger kicking and twisting within her, knowing that the hardest day's work she will ever do is just ahead, and still come into her doctor's office with a smile, is beyond masculine understanding. They have a right to act a *little* queer when the notion strikes them.

10

The Disorganization Woman

A man is in general better pleased when he has a good dinner upon his table than when his wife talks Greek.

SAMUEL JOHNSON

IT IS JUST too bad that women cannot have their wish and all of them remain in their romantic twenties for the next fifty years instead of growing old and acquiring the less attractive qualities which are bound to accompany mature years.

Your twenty year old bride was, of course, as nutty as a pet coon, or at least she took the trouble to make you believe her so. But there was an air of innocence about her antics that made you love her more for her inconsistencies than for her real accomplishments.

Such behavior looks ridiculous in a mature woman of thirty-plus, and somehow your own gift of forgiveness has shrunk in direct proportion to her maturity. Now you expect her to be an equal partner in this enterprise; if she lapses into the state the head shrinkers call "inadequate personality" you are inclined to rear up on your hind feet and paw the air a bit. She cannot understand your attitude, or realize that cute puppy tricks are not appreciated in older dogs. A pup can gnaw holes in your

113

best socks while an older dog begs to be sent to the dog pound for such misdeeds. A wife who puts those same socks in your drawer without an attempt to remedy the damage will hear from you in no uncertain terms.

So the fight is on, and both parties wonder if they did not make a mistake back there someplace while traveling through that rose-tinted fog.

During her twenties your little darling tried with a degree of success to superimpose the image of her dream man onto your bent and inadequate frame, but by thirty she sees you as you really are—a balding, pot-bellied, thin-shanked old goat, with the disposition of the male of that species. A woman just cannot fool herself all the time, and the realistic picture of pop unshaven and exhausted from a hard day at the office is certainly not the answer to a maiden's prayer. She may, as some women do, accept the deuce she drew in the matrimonial shuffle and worry along to the end, or she may begin to compare you to the glamorous males she meets and to dream of what might have been had she chosen some other mate.

Statistics tell us that more unfaithfulness to the marriage vows comes in the third decade of a woman's life than at any other period. In the twenties she still has enough imagination to tint your faults with romance, and in her forties she loses hope and just doesn't give a damn any more. But it is in this period of the thirties that that old savage instinct to breed up instead of down steals into a woman's mind. Not many of them can say they didn't wonder if mating with some more glamorous male would not result in their bringing forth an Einstein or another sex goddess for Hollywood to lend luster to their striving upon this earth. This is more likely to occur if you have shown yourself to be not too successful in the battle for the dollar.

Vance Packard says that women are the most avid status seekers. Being married to an also-ran requires adjustments of girlhood dreams which many a woman is not capable of making. She may have developed into a scratchy old cat, and the metamorphosis from the cute little kitten you married seems intolerable; but stop and consider that perhaps you were the cause of that transformation yourself. Marriage is hard work for both parties and only an old man can sympathize with a husband at this trying time, realizing that life is like that—just a series of compromises with the dreams of boyhood.

Here is another reason why a man should delay venturing into marriage until he has found himself and realized his potentialities: a girl who marries a man of thirty or more knows, when she takes him, about how far he is liable to fly and what she can expect in future years in the way of mink coats, and so forth. With most of us the pattern is fixed by that time, and a creature as calculating as woman can see ahead to just what she is getting into. Besides, she accepts a man for what he is and does not try to remake him into the dreamboy who filled her girlish dreams.

Woman has the original dual personality; she seems to want to have children and care for a home, but then in her thirties she is overwhelmed with a desire to do what Margaret Mead calls "search for her own personality" (which means in plain language that she is tired of domesticity and wants to step out in the world and compete with men on their own ground).

She gave up her name and her individual personality when she married and had children who bore your name. Now she intends to have her name up in lights—her maiden name, if you please, just like the movie stars; she will only accept dual billing if her name comes first. Your name may be Smith and her maiden name Jones, but "The Smiths" will no longer satisfy her; the marriage firm should read "Jones-Smith Corp., Marjorie Jones, President." She will never be satisfied until laws are enacted that will make this combination legal, and probably not then.

No one really knows what women want out of life, and women themselves have less idea than men have. There is only one safe bet: They will want something different from what they have today.

Here I must try to be fair; I must be counsel for the defense as well as for the prosecution. I must defend a woman's right to develop herself into a person separate from a wife and mother, and at the same time show what a hell of a mess she makes of it, particularly from our male standpoint. But can we blame her for her efforts to step out into the world and to try at long last to attain that cherished goal of becoming a "real person" in every sense of the word?

It is a terrible struggle for her, because she is still the half-civilized little feline that came out of the trees slung over Cain's back, though her mate shows little of the savage that made Cain attractive to the Nod maidens. Still she hopes that there may be some other man who has those strictly masculine attributes.

It was, I believe, Dr. Menninger who stated that for every woman patient who complained of her husband's excessive virility, at least a dozen complained about their husbands' relative impotence. Sorry, buddy, but every time you changed those baby diapers, cooked a meal, or washed up the kitchen afterwards, you lost some of your tail feathers and enhanced your abilities to cluck. I know your wife had to help make the living and was too tired to do these things when she got home; nevertheless, ten years later when she states scornfully to her doctor that her mate is little better than a eunuch, you have only yourself to blame. There are no wonder drugs that will restore your lost manhood or keep your wife from envying another woman whose mate limits his household chores to emptying his own ashtrays and paying the bills.

There was a time when you could have avoided all of this domestic misery and dissatisfaction by taking a powder before the minister said the fatal words. Better a crusty old bachelor, buying his sex, than a downtrodden excuse for a man who is unsuccessful in bringing up the rhubarb. And now, to make the matter worse, your secret sorrow is not your own; she will tell it with all the garish details to her medical advisor, and probably at the bridge table too.

Doctors flock together, not because they like their own company better than that of other men—they hate each other—but because the layman never gets on easy terms of comradeship with his physician. He can't because he is all the time wondering just what his wife has told the doc about his masculine attributes. The doctor does not enjoy hearing his fellow men discussed so frankly, but he realizes that he is dealing with a half-wild creature whose ideas of social ethics and the sanctity of the bedroom are still very primitive.

Why do I call her half-wild? I'll be glad to take it all back if you can show me one woman who does not use more paint and mud upon her face than the savages of darkest Africa, to say nothing of the false eyelashes, gaudy ten cent store jewelry, and other forms of decoration so appreciated by those aborigines. She and the cat are two animals who, despite all our efforts to civilize them, have retained their primal instincts unimpaired.

A woman's ideas of adornment are still very primitive.

But, as I hinted before, she also has a brain, and one that is as capable of absorbing learning as any man's. During her thirties she is torn between her savage nature and her desire to equal or surpass man in his own field. One day she wants to be a true female, running her home, being cherished and petted and overwhelmed with masculinity. The next day she frets like a chained coyote because she is not out in the business jungle shooting down her own game, plus a few men for good measure. She is more to be pitied than censured. The more book learning she has acquired before she takes on her role of housewife, the more difficult it is for her to choose between a homebody or a jungle hunter once the rush of child bearing is over. Those long, long years ahead loom up like an endless desert road.

But perhaps you have never traveled upon a desert road in our Western States. You come up over a little hill and the blacktop seems to stretch endlessly on, almost as far as the eye can see, before it winds into another hill similar to the one you have just passed. Between these two points of elevation there is nothing to distract the eye except sage brush and an occasional desert raven flying lazily in the equally uninteresting blue of the sky. The farther you go the more distant the next break in the monotony seems, and you feel like a little bug trying to make his way across a picture window. Your watch seems to lag over the minutes as if each were an eternity. Though you hear the hum of the motor, you are half convinced that this is the end of everything, that the exciting events of your life are all behind you and that the future is as void of interest as the present landscape.

All right, smarty, just what would you advise your wife to do in this bleak situation? If two weeks vacation about drives *you* nuts, try and think what forty years of idleness must look like to her. But our entire economic effort for the last fifty years has been devoted to the principle that to make our wives happy we must provide them with more and more expensive gadgets to relieve them of the drudgery of housekeeping. The most perfect and efficient animal organism ever created is doomed to a life of luxurious nothing because her man cherishes the idea that she is a poor, weak bean vine that must cling to him for support and fulfill her destiny of being an ornament reflecting his success in life's battle. And she, poor creature, is willing to nourish this hallucination. She knows that if she shows herself more intelligent and versatile than man, he will be repelled by her apparent superiority (and he definitely will be, no question about that).

There is the problem. There are not enough little home bodies who have to take off their shoes to count above ten to go around, so it looks like the honored custom of marriage is doomed. The only solution I can see is to castrate all the less likely males, stand the others at stud, turn the running of the world over to the women and let them work this thing out as best they can.

This section is based on findings of female psychologists, so we will have to forsake the rational explanations for your wife's conduct and trust in these ladies to guide us. After all, they are women and should know what they are talking about.

You will find some of this mixed-up information about your wife in the book *The Second Sex,* by Miss Simone deBeauvior, which is acknowledged to be one of the best studies of female psychology in print today. But it is as long as *Gone With the Wind,* and not half so interesting.

They tell us that when confronting men, women are always acting, and we must agree that if this is so they sure do a good job of it. Your girlfriend feels so frustrated in the evident fact that she is not a man that she hates the sex, you included. But she can't afford to show it, and so trys to show her mastery of the brute by sweetly talking you into getting married. I have only seen one man who would acknowledge that he proposed marriage to his wife, and he considers himself a horrible example and has always regretted his hasty actions.

The marriage ceremony is degrading to the female because she feels like a stray kitten that her dad is giving away to some strange man because he has more of them than he can handle about the house. They tell us that marriage makes women into praying mantes, leaches and poisonous creatures. Wives want to hold their mates while resisting their domination and every one of them has to battle the rest of the world to preserve the situation that dooms her to dependence.

So right off the bat you must understand that your pride and joy married you to get even with you; instead of being a partner down through the years she is even more anxious to see you get a kick in the pants, providing she is the kicker. I must acknowledge that there is a cruel streak in most women, and the more feminine they are the more it is in evidence. Following is a true story to illustrate my point.

I was working as a railway telegrapher, and my relief was a kind, thoughtful, and good looking youngster who unfortunately was innocent of the tricks of females. He was much in love with a young lady who was a pillar in the church and, to hear her tell it, one of the co-authors of the Golden Rule. He asked me to work part of his shift one night that he might take this paragon to the county fair. When he finally showed up to relieve me, his depression was so thick I could hardly recognize the boy. It seemed that at the fair his girl had seen another of her chums loafing in front of the monkey cage, and called out and asked her to join them in making the rounds. This was repeated several times. Things were so set up that not always did the invitation come from his lady friend, but he himself was forced to issue it, or act like a hog. He noted that *she* guided *him* about the grounds, and realized that the other girls, all without escorts, had been briefed on where to be found. Before he got back he had spent two weeks' wages taking that bunch of sap-suckers into all the side shows and on every ride at the fair.

"I wouldn't feel nearly so bad," he said, "but when I took off my coat I found 'Easy' written in chalk upon the back in letters a foot high."

That boy went on to a prominent position in railroading, but the girl married a farmer and had to work like the dickens, which served her damn well right. This prank cheated her out of mink stoles and all that goes with the position of the wife of a successful executive. But she had a brief moment of triumph when she showed the other girls just how easy it was for her to make a man spend his money.

But back to Miss deBeauvoir. Another pearl of wisdom from the pen of this illustrious French woman is that good house-keepers are the cold type; only the messy, pack-rat type of woman is adequate in the performance of her marital gymnastics. So forget your dreams of a neat little nest with a loving wife; you can have one, but not the other. "You pays your money and you takes your choice."

The lady also states that marriage is only a surviving relic of a dead way of life. So why don't we men band together and refuse to go through with such nonsense? If women want so badly to be equal, why not let them? Somehow we always believed it was the *man* who had to give up so many pleasures when he assumed the yoke of family life.

Women have been yelling about their rights for a hundred years. Yesterday I read a letter from the funny man Artemus Ward, published in a newspaper a hundred years ago, and he told the same old story that is so prominent among our female thinkers today. I thought we had long ago given women all the rights they wanted, but let us go the whole hog and give them the rest of those they seem to crave.

Let's abolish marriage as a religious and moral institution, and make it a simple contract. But let's first insist that along with the father giving away the bride, the mother of the groom stands on the other side and gives away her darling son to this conniving creature who has stolen his wits. That would indeed make a ridiculous rite, and the contractual form would be readily adopted in its stead by the girls.

Make the contract read for one year, with a renewal clause on option, up to the time when babies appear. Then increase the time of the contract to extend fifteen years after the birth of the youngest child. Each partner should, upon voiding the contract, take out his original financial investment; any moneys accumulated during the time of the contract should be divided equally. Alimony be abolished and only expenses of education of the children should be shared equally after the contract has been voided. The wife should retain her maiden name and the kids allowed to assume whatever name they desired at the age of fifteen. That would surely satisfy the female's desire for the development of her own personality, and make her a partner in the business rather than an inside competitor. Besides, using her own name she could not write checks on your account, which will make most men in favor of woman's rights, I'm sure.

With all of these masculine rights, she surely will at last be willing to give up her privileges. It will not be considered boorish to walk in front of her going through a door or getting on a bus. You won't have to rise when she comes into a room or approaches a dining table.

Any way you look at it, we men can only gain by insisting that woman exercise the rights she has and be endowed with all the rest of them. We may have to change the babies, but that seems to be the established custom among the younger set now, so all of the gains would be in the masculine favor.

A question arises, however; could we induce her to accept all of this freedom? For generations she enjoyed being man's darling, and has done very well for herself in the role of his vassal. She has had the unique opportunity of being both servant and master. But she may be difficult to convince that equal rights plus equal responsibilities are to be preferred to the exalted position she now occupies. And the more feminine her nature, the more stubborn she is likely to be.

Miss deBeauvoir makes one statement with which I most heartily agree. She says that women who grow up under the influence of the father rather than the mother are a much easier type to get along with; they see things from a more masculine viewpoint, practice less deception, and are not all the time trying to impress upon the male that they are poor helpless little kittens instead of scheming cats. So I warn you, if you would have peace and satisfaction in your married state, either marry a woman who idolized her father and tried to be like him, or expend your best efforts toward that glorious day when woman will at last get her rights and be free.

The ideal woman, from a man's point of view, is of course the one who, as her children take up less and less of her time and enegry, directs her attention to their father. She kindles the fires of love and admiration all over again, and so goes down through the valley hand in hand with her husband.

Unfortunately, it takes much more patience and skill to rekindle an old fire than to start a new one, and there always seems to be somebody ready with paper and matches to assist one or the other partner in starting a real conflagration. Then the singed victims wind up in the divorce court.

But believe it or not, there are women who, from the day they say "I do" to the end of their lives, respect and love their husbands. They put the children into a secondary position and gain the eternal romance. You may be lucky, but I doubt if you are lucky enough to get one of these; they come straight from Heaven and spend no time in yearning to be personalities. They consider themselves a part of a team that is supposed to face the world together.

Then there are the women who take up bridge seriously, and those who never read a book except best seller sex novels. These are the counterpart of the eternal sophomore in the male, and their claims of intellectual superiority are even more revolting than his childish pranks.

Some women go back to school and honestly try to resume the life of the career girl, but the great majority become skillful and adroit in giving the impression that they are busy and happy while perfecting themselves in the noble old art of loafing.

This wild woman of thirty-plus is in the same quandary as newly freed small nations; she wants to go forward and throw off the sheltered life her mother led, develop her personality, reduce men to baby-sitters, run the country and the world, and still she wants a strong right arm and shoulder to fly back to when the going gets rough. When she feels like being babied, she wants some male around to baby her.

How women are going to combine the two sides of their nature I do not know, nor does any other man, but as usual their plight is all our fault. We have used our inventive brains to make cute household gadgets and work-savers for them instead of inventing missiles as we should have been doing. We have made our automobiles so long and luxurious that they resemble ladies' drawing rooms, and so big there is no place to park them. In short, we have tried to make life as glamorous as was possible and now we find that too many of the good things in life are even more boring than slums and poverty.

The business life of our country is based upon the assumption that we can persuade women to demand more and more of things that add not one grain of ultimate satisfaction to their lives. Our prosperity depends upon inadequate personalities, which means, among other things, an inability to resist the blandishments of the advertiser and to buy everything that is offered whether we have any need for it or not.

There is another pitfall which these status-seeking, career-chasing wives may push you into; and it is being nagged to death. It is most damnable of all their peculiar feminine tricks. A man is so constituted that he must have someone to believe in him to succeed at anything. I have seen good men ruined due to their wives nagging because the status symbols were not accumuating fast enough. When a woman makes up her mind that her husband is a failure, and informs him of the fact, he becomes, in a majority of cases, a failure indeed. If she has no confidence in his abilities he soon adopts her point of view, and almost at once his fellows accept his conclusions and he is considered a dud when promotions are being passed around. His wife defeats her own desires and ruins his life by harping on the fact that the neighbors have a newer model car than he does, that Mary's husband has his name on the office door and poor old John does not.

There is nothing more depressing for a doctor than trying to treat a man who has lost his tail feathers; such a patient develops symptoms of every disease in the book and is more difficult to help because he subconsciously doesn't want to get well.

I once knew a guy who was so henpecked and depressed that the seat of his pants dragged on the ground and obliterated his footprints. But when the grim reaper mowed down his old harpy, he married a girl who spent a major portion of her time boosting his ego. The change in that man and the way his fellows regarded him was close to a miracle.

I once advised a girl against marriage to a boy who had shown no signs of ever getting any place or wanting to do so. She didn't take my advice, and in ten years that man was a leader in his work and circle of friends. My diagnosis was wrong because I failed to recognize her potential.

A lifetime of practicing medicine has convinced me that the

Learn to hold on to your tailfeathers for a time.

woman a man marries has more to do with his success or failure
than the man himself. I made a lot of home calls, and when I
was called to a new family I did not inquire into the man's
credit rating or job prospects. I looked around the house and so
made up my mind whether I wanted to have this family's professional business or not. If the house, poor though it might be,
was clean, the wife neat and cheerful, the children happy, I
extended them all the credit and time they needed, even if the
man seemed to be just a stick-in-the-mud. On the other hand,
no matter how glamorous the husband's job and prospects, if
his wife was a sloppy housekeeper and a whiner, I got out of
the picture as quickly as possible, instinctively knowing that she
would spend more money than he could make, and my services
would probably go unpaid. When I retired from the active
practice of medicine there wasn't a thousand dollars of bad
debts on my books, so I guess my queer way of credit rating
paid off.

We hear a lot these days about big heartless corporations
investigating the wife of the applicant, as well as the man himself. I don't know what their standards are in regard to wives,
but I applaud their interest in the distaff side of the family.
But if I were the personnel man I would conduct the survey in

the home instead of at the cocktail party or office. I've seen some awful tramps made to look like queens at these clambakes, and heard them publicly butter up their husbands as if they were saints. But I was a doctor, and medicine unfortunately requires that you know the home environment as well as physical symptoms before you can evaluate many cases.

There are many things other than textbook diseases that affect a patient's well being; in fact I believe that fifty per cent of the people who come into a doctor's office are suffering from conditions that wonder drugs and diagnostic machines cannot cure or even discover. It is surprising the number of people one sees who have a subconscious desire for death and are secretly happy if you find something that might contribute to their hasty end. This is, I believe, more common in women than in men, and sometimes the doctor has a struggle with his Hippocratic oath to avoid abetting them in their desire to get out of a hopeless situation.

I remember one case in which the woman, an admirable character, was married to a brute of a man. He was a shiftless, no-good sort of a cuss who thought his only marital duty was to keep his woman pregnant and let the community provide for the results thereof. While I was delivering her twelfth child, she had a severe post-partum hemorrhage. The nurse and I worked like dogs to save her, but before the hemorrhage had been checked she had lapsed into unconsciousness. Finally, when we were successful in stopping the blood and had restored the fluid balance in her vascular system, she came out of it and began to cry.

"Oh why did you do this cruel thing to me? I seemed to be floating off on the softest bed, and now you've brought me back to a world of pain and hopelessness. Sometimes you doctors are most cruel when you are trying to be kind. I have prayed long and faithfully that I might be taken, and but for your meddling I would have been."

The hell of it was, I knew she meant it. An old midwife used to say, "There are a lot worse things than death in this world," and she was so right.

Dr. Cabot, the great heart specialist of an earlier day, used to tell the story of a dear little old lady who came to him, much troubled because of the way her family was treating her. They seemed to be eternally watching her and trying to do things for her that she preferred doing for herself. He explained that because of her physical condition he had warned the children that she might die suddenly. They were most anxious to make her last days as pleasant as possible, and by relieving her of her accustomed duties hoped to postpone the fatal outcome. She replied, "Oh, is *that* all. I was afraid they thought I was going crazy." She left happy and smiling; death had no fears for her like those of becoming mentally deranged.

It's these ladies that can take all the guff we men hand out who deserve the laurel leaves. And like as not your own sweetie will win more than you'd imagine after she's completed a lifetime with you.

In this thirtyish period she may howl about rights and dig into her subconscious (and yours, too) searching for personality, but let her have her fun. She won't be happy until she does, and she'll drive you crazy if she doesn't. Give her enough rope and she'll hang herself. Then, if you are quick, you can cut down the body before the last gasp and breathe your own way of thinking into the more pliable remains.

All the rights she really wanted in the first place were those of calling you Lord and Master in all honesty, and of developing her own personality in the way that suits you best. So if you'll just hold on to your tail feathers for a time, you can reorganize the lady, and she'll love you for it.

11

The Career Woman— and You Can Have Her

Because of their vices, women have ceased to deserve the privileges of their sex; they have put off their womanly nature and are therefore condemned to suffer the diseases of men.

SENECA

A WOMAN AT the age of thirty-five has no more idea about what she wants to make of her life than the girl of ten, but even the dumbest of husbands should, after fifteen years of marriage, be able to anticipate some of her future actions and to know what manner of woman she is. The procreative urge has somewhat cooled within her little head, and though it may suffer a resurgence as she nears the close of her fruitful period in the early forties, at thirty-five she is distinctly cool to the idea of another offspring.

At this time all women can be roughly classified into two categories: domestic and worldly Have-gots, and similar Have-nots.

The first general classification depends upon finances: have you arrived at this point with plenty of money, or are you burdened with debts and two or three children to see through college? If you are a Have-got and your little wife is at heart a domestic individual whose entire world begins and ends with her husband and children, you are lucky. She will never dream of forsaking the now nearly empty nest, but will devote all of her spare time to making it an attractive place for husband and children to come home to. She is probably interested in the eternal struggle of women to achieve their own personalities independent of their married state, but only as a spectator. She finds her outlet in the lives of those dearest to her, and will sacrifice her own desires and wishes that they may prosper, just as does the mother bird with a nest full of hungry mouths. She is not a stimulating individual when met at a party or a club meeting because she considers most such things merely vanities, of secondary importance in the business of living. In this day and age she is somewhat of a rarity, and if discovered should be admired with reverence.

The other great branch of women in this general classification of Have-gots consists of a very different breed of cats. Fundamentally they are vain, lazy, and selfish to an astonishing degree. They find many interests to take the place of the forced domesticity of the earlier years, and proceed to fill up their new-found leisure with cocktail parties, fashion shows, beauty parlors, and shopping trips. When they have a troubled feeling in the region where their conscience is supposed to be, they usually join a cockeyed movement for the betterment of something. The cause makes little difference; the lady of leisure only looks to see which glamorous movie star is heading the organization, and whether the local members are listed in the town's *Who's Who*. If she manages to peck her way to the near top of this clique, she remains a shining light in such good works; otherwise to hell with it. She is that dame you see frequenting the lobbies of fancy hotels and darkened cocktail bars, decked out in a thousand dollars worth of clothes, no more expression on her face than a turnip plastered over with a small fortune in cosmetics. She is just a plain high class tramp, who is only waiting for a coronary occlusion or the divorce court to relieve her of the burden of her husband. She is eager for her rightful inheritance so she can move to Europe, where society is so much more glamorous. This specimen is much more numerous than the domestic little hen, and has truly "developed her personality." When she dies she can do so with a clear conscience, never having done anything in her life that wasn't motivated by selfishness. How I will enjoy painting her picture as an old lady in a future chapter.

Now we come to a much larger grouping—the Have-nots—wives whose husbands have not been able to clear the family of debts by the time they have reached the thirty-fifth milestone. These women are restrained by circumstances and a lingering vestige of that definition of woman as a helpmeet for her husband. This type of woman is happy to get a job where she can have some outside interest, and still do her housework on evenings and holidays. She is the most dependable help that it is possible to obtain.

Young women are probably much more decorative in an office or place of business; but like the stallion in a horse race, they don't keep their minds on their business. About the time one feels that he has one of them trained in the office routine, along comes a boy and she walks off without even a "glad to have met you."

With the older working woman, romance is just a smouldering ember rather than the fierce flame of romantic love. But according to statistics those embers can be rekindled easily, and the igniting spark is boredom. There seems to be a much greater tendency to female infidelity at this age than at any other, and authorities would have us believe that it is due to an unstable mental attitude. Of course an unstable mentality is just another way of saying "female," so that has nothing to do with it. Some people get bored more easily than others; those who avoid this curse are people with no imagination at all. Some women, like a lot of men, will risk anything on a gamble —be it love, horse racing or slot machines. The fun is in the doing, and damn the consequence.

The great majority of these older women, however, take a serious view of their jobs and try their best to give a dollar's worth of service for the dollar in the pay envelope. This is why, when you go into a department store with your wife, you see the glamour girls on the first floor selling jewelry and knickknacks, but when you reach the dress and hat departments the clerks are more elderly ladies. The sweet young things just don't have the patience to put up with the indecisions of the customer shopping for a hat; besides, they seldom see men in the upper departments unless it is some henpecked old goat who was just brought along because his wife had no convenient place to check him.

The henpecked old goat was brought along because his wife had no convenient place to check him.

The older woman who has experience in running a house will quickly identify herself with her job and the firm, and will, incidentally, try to run the whole show. But you can't have everything.

There is only one class of mature female help that does not conform to the pattern of steadiness described above, and that is married nurses. When girls go into nursing they all plan to marry doctors before they graduate, and then they forget all about the picture of Florence Nightingale. But there are not enough doctors to go around, and somehow nursing destroys all the natural sagacity born into a woman. They wind up married to the worst bunch of tramps and philanderers they can find. Just when you think you have found a jewel of a nurse, her hubby goes off on a big drunk with some floosy and your jewel has to give up her job and go back home to try and civilize this infant before the police catch up with him. Of course this doesn't always happen, but it happens often enough to constitute a pattern.

As a rule the married helper of this age is dependable, interested in her job, and inclined to confine her bitching to the home circle, an admirable employee and a true friend.

So your wife has reached the halfway mark in her journey and is thirty-five years old. She has been raising so much hell the last year that now you have given in and agreed to her going out into the world in search of that illusive thing called, by the women writers upon the subject, her own personality. You have had your say, but as usual been overruled. The business world, as well as those of finance and the arts, had better tighten up their belts and get ready to be reorganized.

This is going to be a rare and enjoyable period for you, but please don't ride too hard on that most hateful of all phrases, "I told you so." Of course she isn't going to like it, and there will be much threatening weather and some storms. But you will infuriate her more by taking the side of the company boss than if you sympathize with her. It is only human to blame all of her miscarried plans upon someone else; if she lands in an office, it is the lady office manager who is jealous of her and fears that she is going to steal her job; if she is a sales lady, she gets all the hard customers and everybody above her in the pecking line is a double dyed you-know-what.

The big wheel is her ideal; she is eternally comparing his clothes and manners with your own. She goes through that painful but enlightening experience of becoming, or hoping to become, an office wife; then all of her barbed shots are directed toward her lawful wedded one. This lasts a month or two and then one morning he comes in grouchy as a bear, with a sore head or with a gleam in his eye, and either bawls her out good for some trivial error or invites her to go on a business trip with him. Either one will destroy this idol quickly and completely. She will begin hinting around that it was all *your* fault; you drove her out of her cozy little home because you wanted more money to play the horses.

Don't get sore and start a fuss, give this calf enough rope and she will surely soon realize that she is the most bored person on the block and home will again seem the glamorous place that she once thought it was. When she discovers that career women are the most dissatisfied people on earth she will be happy to resume her position as homemaker and make up her mind to grow old gracefully.

The married or single woman who has reached the age of thirty-five without bearing children is an entirely different individual. She has had so much time to develop her own personality that she is disgusted with the whole business. She feels that nature and circumstances have robbed her of her birthright.

In business the career woman, even more than the career male, is a misfit and knows it. The success she has in the world of masculine business is a bore, much more so than washing dishes and changing diapers. And nature has some more dirty tricks up her sleeve for this barren female. If she hasn't used her uterus for the purpose for which it was installed within her, she finds that at about this age it begins to grow. So she turns out like the lady in the old patent medicine song: "There was a kind lady, and she had a tumor sore, so she took two bottles of compound, and now has two tumors more." At this point she must undergo surgery, and so the seed is removed from the grape. This, unlike the natural menopause, causes her personality to store up vinegar and she becomes somewhat critical of her associates and surroundings. She is the best of workers, gets ulcers like any other junior executive, and must be treated with a lot more deference and consideration than the woman who has fulfilled her function and is as calm and collected as a gestating cow.

The career woman's ambition to become a grey-flannel-suited captain of industry has floundered on the rocks of sex. Her ultimate achievement seems to be limited to bossing a dozen or so giddy young secretaries who despise her and show it at every opportunity. So she develops gallstones, migraine headaches, and a disposition like a roll of barbed wire. She may wear the most glamorous of clothes, but there is no more unhappy female upon the face of the earth (unless it is a divorcée with too much money to spend).

Women are too intense in their emotions ever to be able to cope with the business world without a decided change in their personalities; they are too prone to tire of a job and go looking for a greener pasture to make much of a success of a career. They are all individualists, and team play, unless they are the head of the team, is a dreary bore. Of course there are exceptions; so are there white-breasted robins—but they are rare compared with the number of birds hatched.

But bless their hearts, they just must develop that career type personality, and it takes them fifty or more years to realize that the woman with the real personality is the one who creates a home for her family and carries it on to the final round. The homebody has outside interests of course, but they are not competing with men in partnership with other women.

There is something about marriage and bearing children that fulfills a woman's life and character, as well as that of the father of the brood. Bachelor ladies, like their opposite number, are much more difficult people to live with, though they are also the most efficient individuals in any business organization.

To understand human nature we must look to nature's way as demonstrated by the acts of other inhabitants of this earth. Man is the smartest of them all, of course, because he has been able to invent ways to kill both for sport and to fulfill his so-called patriotic duty. He was cursed at birth with an inability to be satisfied with his lot, and has spent his whole existence trying to change his environment. How do we know that building an air ship or a TV camera would have been an impossibility for a cow, had she been born with as restless and unhappy a disposition as man's? Who can prove that a female politician, business leader, or actress is more happy with her lot than the mother robin incubating a bunch of eggs and breaking her back feeding the baby birds once they arrive?

Did you ever see an unhappy lady robin, or one who was divorced? Probably not, but I once was given the opportunity to watch the breakup in a robin's dreams of home and family. I guess the wife was destined to be one of these career females. She was evidently a new bride and had never before coped with the nest building chore. Early in the spring she picked out a spot in a shade tree right in front of our cottage door. Hubby sat upon the topmost branch and declared to all the world that this was his territory, fought off the jay birds, and was most dutiful in bringing her sticks and straw. She required a lot of material; her first effort looked as if it belonged to an eagle and was big enough to accommodate a family of them. It fell to the lawn below and I cleaned up the mess. She tried again, and again she showed herself no home architect; it wound up the same way. The third time she almost made it. Her perseverance was paying off, but just as she was putting on the finishing touches it followed the rest.

By this time I had accumulated a stack of nest building material bigger than a bushel basket. Like the poor robin husband, I was beginning to get a bit disgusted. After the second failure he seemed to lose his voice, and after the third failure he walked out on her and was not seen again. She hung around the tree for a spell, then seemed to tire of the neighborhood, and left for parts unknown. I have seen the same scene enacted many times in the human family; the female either did not know how to build a home, or felt that the job was a menial occupation and gave her no opportunity to develop her personality.

Frankly I do not believe any single person ever develops a real personality; it is the union of the male and female that is a personality. A family personality and a complete life is graphically illustrated by the great seal of my native state of Missouri. It shows two bears holding up a globe with the legend "United we stand; divided we fall." Unfortunately most of us who do not keep that motto in mind when we go forth to achieve that illusive goal of developing our personalities and making ourselves a power in the world. Longfellow put the thing nicely:

As unto the bow the cord is; so unto the man is woman;
Though she bends him, she obeys him,
Though she draws him, yet she follows;
Useless each without the other!

But your wife just must buckle on her armor and go forth to slay the dragon of housewifely mediocrity. Let's look at some of the jobs she holds and the rewards therefrom. Suppose she finds employment as a bank teller; she will be on her feet all day developing fallen arches, handling filthy old money and worried every minute that she might dish out one too many twenty dollar bill, knowing good and well that the customer rarely calls her attention to such a slip. When she figures up her deductions, taxes, and cost of suitable raiment for the job, plus a baby sitter or cleaning woman at home, she will find that the return is like that of the old dance hall manager in a little town. Too many people came to listen to the music and didn't pay to dance, so he closed up shop remarking, "These dances amount to more than they come to."

Should she take up general office work and spend her days at a typewriter, all she gets out of it is a stenographer's spread instead of fallen arches, and any woman would prefer flat feet to a flat and wide rear exposure. Perhaps she teaches school, sells insurance, or works in a factory, it's all the same; after three weeks the job is as boring as making the holes in Swiss cheese.

There is nothing in this world that does not become a task and a mighty bore if we feel that we are forced to do it so that we may retain our economic position in society. The only antidote is a feeling of accomplishment, the belief that we have added something to the comfort of the world in general, and that our individual contribution is such that no one else could have filled our place.

Eric Fromm says men and women are growing more alike every day simply because they are both growing more like machines. May I add: just who dreams of being married to a machine?

You should try to understand the lady's problems and do what you can to make life interesting, but never let her take a job that pays more than yours does. If she gets that sort of a break, divorce her at once; it saves many a heartache in the future.

It is well if your chosen bride has some skill developed so that if she were widowed she could support herself, but before the knot is tied have an understanding that you are to be the breadwinner and she is to be the baker. You may be growing more like a machine every day, but try to develop yourself so that you will remain a ball-bearing mechanism and not a simple abacus. The time will come when she demands the right to step out and become a personality, but if she is worth having she will soon tire of that and reassume her proper role as one-half of the partnership.

You may never be happy, but who is? A long time ago Seneca said, "To be happy, add not to your possessions but subtract from your desires." Our Twentieth Century economy is based upon exactly the opposite philosophy; be discontented with what you have and strive to acquire things you have no earthly use for, just to impress people whom you don't like anyhow. Go further and further in debt for these unnecessary gadgets and see that your government does the same. Strive hard for notoriety and acclaim, and let your wife do the same in the development of her personality. Like Solomon, you will some day awake to the fact that it is all vanity anyhow, and as useless and unsatisfactory as last year's bird nests.

For both of you it is the little things that count—the kindness toward each other and humanity in general. And there is also the raising of children that you can be proud of, and the sacrifices you endured that they might be well prepared for life, able to judge between right and wrong, between the gold of simple things and the brass of sham and pretense. The development of a personality boils down to "Do unto others as you would be done by."

So now you have the female as she reaches thirty-five; decide

She strives to acquire things she has no earthly use for.

In which category your pride and joy fits, and govern yourself accordingly. If she wants to work, let her; she misses the kids that have grown up and left the nest and she just must have something to do to occupy her thoughts and bodily energies. If she is childless, you are spared the decision—she will be working anyhow. If she is a gentle little homebody who thinks ninety-nine cents is so much cheaper than a dollar, get down on your knees at night and thank God for the many blessings bestowed upon you.

12

She's Two Score and She's A Tiger

Thyself no more deceive, thy youth hath fled.
PETRARCH

Your wife is now reaching the gloomy forties and you feel that you are an old experienced husband and have endured everything in the art of living with a female.

Brother, you are just out of kindergarten; the next few years hold some surprises for you about which you never dreamed. . . .

The poet described budding womanhood as a girl child standing with reluctant feet where the brook and river meet. He could just as well have continued that analogy thirty years later and showed the woman standing with even more reluctant feet where the river runs into the ocean.

However, the Twentieth Century has its own descriptive literature, so we will compare woman at this time of crisis with a satellite that has been orbiting around the earth for some forty years, and whose battery is about spent. The future seems, to her at least, to be that of a bit of cosmic junk due to orbit in obscurity until time and gravity draw it close enough to be destroyed in the atmosphere. Her physical mission accomplished or not, nature draws the string and no more messages of romance will emanate from her wildly beating heart. Her vascular control center functions erratically so that she swings from hot to cold with unreasonable rapidity. Her metabolism slows down and everything she eats seemingly turns to fat. The menopause is not a pleasant prospect.

Though she may lie about her age, have her face lifted, insist that gauze be draped over the TV camera lens, dye her hair and wear youthful styles in dress, still she knows that she cannot hold the clock back one single hour. Luckily she is made of different material than her mate, or social security would lose half of its customers.

We read about the male climacteric and some authorities claim that he goes through the same set of bodily shocks, but no man will acknowledge that such things have ever occurred in his lifetime. And each and every man of seventy firmly believes that, given the right partner, he could reproduce his kind as well as when he was twenty-one. From the prevalence of newspaper accounts of men of ninety fathering children, we must accept his claims, even while speculating upon the helpfulness of his neighbors.

I have often wondered just what would happen if suddenly all men of forty were confronted with the certainty that in another five years they would lose that gift from the gods that makes them men. The hot flashes, mental earthquakes and physical changes that affect the female would seem mild indeed compared with the convulsions of nature generated by the male under similar circumstances. I would hate to be a physician in such a time. Listening to the wailing of women would be child's play, and added to the din created by one's male customers would be the awful knowledge that one had to go through the same syndrome himself. The entire male population would be in the funny house by the time they were forty years old just worrying about it.

At least you, the husband of a woman in her early forties, can imagine yourself in her place, and surely you will develop understanding and sympathy for her predicament. And it is indeed a time for understanding, even though you, being a man, can in no way appreciate that dark cloud appearing on her mental horizons.

For you life may not exactly begin at forty, but it loses none of its zest. You are nearing the high point in your career, the silver of age and wisdom is beginning to make itself noticed around the hairline, and you find it convenient to play with your horn-rimmed spectacles when making a speech. (What a wonderful help those things are. I can well remember in the old days when a man arose to talk at a club meeting, he began by rearranging the drinking glasses and silverware on the table before him. It was a sure sign of embarrassment and made everybody else feel uncomfortable. Now he can fool with those new glasses, putting them on, sticking them in his breast pocket, pulling them out and using them as a pointer, and even polishing them on his napkin. Because we see our national leaders doing the same on TV, we feel that such a substitute for napkin twisting is a sign of distinction.) Since it is next to impossible to cover the shine of a bald head in pictures, wigs are becoming fashionable again, and if your hairline is receding too fast you don a youthful looking thatch (crew cut preferred) and the girls smile at you even as they did when you were thirty. In fact their smiles are even wider because you are probably better able to afford expensive presents and are not so choosy as to the attractiveness of the smiler.

Your wife, on the other hand, knows that any admiring glances she gathers will come from burned out old goats of sixty, and if on the odd chance a younger and more glamorous man looks in her direction, his motive is more likely to be financial gain rather than pure romance. And this is more of a blow to her personal ego than if he hadn't smiled at all.

Is it any wonder that your wife becomes disillusioned and disgusted with the whole human race, you in particular? You wonder why, now that there is no danger of consequences, she seems to lose interest in sexual union. It looks to you like a time of unrestrained romance, and her lack of interest whets your appetite for younger and more passionate females.

But woman is a born gambler, and once the chance of getting

Wigs are becoming fashionable again.

pregnant is removed, she is bound to look upon her wifely duties as a chore rather than a recreation. When this great natural game of chance is denied her, she just must gamble with other things. This explains why the slot machines in Nevada are monoplized by gray-haired women; they have given up the sex game and must have an artificial gambling thrill to make their lives bearable. They never leave the casinos with any money; if they get a jackpot they put the loot right back into another machine. They don't play for money, just for the thrill of pulling that lever to see what may happen.

So with your wife's change in body functions fast approaching, try to understand that she must devote her energies to some supplementary pursuits. She still hopes that middle age isn't as bad as it's pictured, and that there is a grain of romance still present in all the chaff of mature woman's activities.

One of the first experiments she tries is acting, and because Hollywood is so blind to talents such as hers she takes advantage of her captive audience and treats you to some fancy performances. If you mention that she forgot to salt the spinach she will sail off into high tragedy with all the gestures of Loretta Young and Helen Hayes jumbled up together. If this makes no impression except to win her the derisive comment "Ham," she may fall back upon woman's old standby—hysterics. Any old hen can fall on the floor, get stiff all over and scream that she is going to die, with telling effect upon both you and her neighbors.

I well remember an instance when a very good friend and patient called in the middle of the night and asked me, as a personal favor, to come and see the wife of one of his renters. She claimed to have taken poison. He was sure that death was imminent and guaranteed the fee, so I went. When I arrived the patient was lying flat on her bed, apparently most gone from this world. As I leaned over to smell her breath to see if I could recognize the drug, she came to life suddenly and grabbed my face, sticking both thumbs into my mouth and trying to stretch my kind old visage out of shape. I tried to bite, but she was smart enough to have inserted her thumbs between my teeth and cheeks. I uncorked an upper cut, with all my body and soul behind it, and connected with the point of her chin. It was the only time I ever struck a woman, but I put all my pent-up desires into that one punch. She took the count of ten all right, and we finally revived her. Then she threw in the towel and spilled the whole story. She had swallowed two aspirin, telling her husband they were strychnine. It all stemmed for his refusal to acknowledge that he had been romancing a girl next door, which investigation proved not to be the case.

My lips didn't get back to normal for several days, and every time I had to shave over the sore spots I was sorry that I hadn't acquired some of Joe Louis' abilities. There is reason in all things, and far be it from me to deny a woman her rights to pull a stunt of some kind to gain her point, but to pick on a doctor who was there to help her was just a little too much. I have never regretted my actions.

If your little woman is not situated at a convenient Nevada gambling spot or Hollywood film lot, she directs her drive along other channels which to you seem equally time wasting. She tries to lose herself in the rush of uplift societies and world betterment movements. This is a most laudable ambition if it is carried out in direct relation to the needs of humanity, but she judges these things in a way that is most mysterious to the masculine mind. Instead of joining a group that is dedicated to the welfare of mankind she picks those organizations that boast of the big names. Status seeker to the last breath, she just must belong to a society that is attractive to the *best* people (meaning, of course, those women who have a change of mink stoles and drive a car that is a cut above the old jalopy which furnishes your transportation).

The cause is of little importance; she can work up as much enthusiasm over a group dedicated to the advancement of cat breeding or raising bigger tuberous begonias as one whose aim is the relief of suffering children. She goes hog wild over this new outlet for her personality, and in the process neglects most shamefully the man she promised to cherish and to cleave unto. I have known women who became so engrossed in these so-called "female personality outlets" that they were hardly ever home when the old man got back from work. When they did get there, they spent the rest of the evening telephoning some of the other hens. They had to discuss plans for the next meeting and some other social climber who scored a beat at the day's gatherings by wearing a hat unlike anything ever seen on a woman's head before.

So Father has to warm up his own TV dinner and amuse himself with the dog and the paper until bedtime. It is little wonder that he toys with the idea of the pleasures connected with taking some chick out to dinner in a dimly-lighted, romantic little spot where the League of Women Voters or the Garden Club will never enter the conversation.

We tend to shudder at the spectacle of an old goat who has shaved off his whiskers, polished up his horns, and splashed himself with some stuff which is guaranteed to make him smell like the piney woods or a burning lumber yard (a scent that the TV advertisers swear is irresistible to the female sex). He looks and acts like an ass, and we rightfully blame it upon some woman's influence. Men are strange creatures, and one of their strangest traits is a preference for dining by candlelight with some chick where the condition of the political world is never mentioned. Arguing over the respective sex appeal of the Democratic and Republican candidates at the breakfast table at home simply can't compare. No man ever married a woman because of her grasp of the international situation. Many an erring husband was driven to his romantic escapades, not by the chick who happens to be his companion, but by his Henny Penny wife who is rushing about trying to prevent the world from falling down. The ladies can be as political minded as they please, but they should find some other outlet for their arguments besides their husbands. We respect their opinions upon all subjects except finance, sports and politics. They used to be able to act dumb on occasions, why have they forgotten the art?

Once a woman is bitten by this club woman hysteria, her own little nest is of minor importance; that is, until someone tells her about Daddy-o's romantic adventures. This emergency separates the women from the female vampire bats. If she ever was a real woman, she rushes to her medical adviser for counsel and help in this domestic emergency; if she belonged to the bat family, as sad to say a lot of them do, she goes to her attorney and insists that he fleece poor old George out of every last cent he possesses.

I have often wondered just what would happen if, by some error in the legal processes, an old experienced family doctor was appointed to the post of judge of a family relations court. He would never serve more than one term—the lawyers and the women on the make would tend to that little detail. But while he was there some of his rulings would make history and front page reading for the rest of the males who might see the published accounts of the court's decisions.

Now I want to be fair about this club business and acknowledge that I do know little about the workings of the various ladies' societies connected with the churches, though most of

the projects I heard about were in connection with some clam-
bake to buy new robes for the choir, or pulpit decorations to
match the minister's hair. However there is one such society that
will always remain enshrined in my memory as a real blessing
to suffering humanity, and that is the Relief Society of the Mormon Church.

Mormon women are females just like Gentiles, much given to
barking up the wrong tree and rushing around in circles trying
to elevate humanity by cultivating homemade ceramics and
such, but they are also taught from the cradle to come running
when the church authorities call. In thirty years of practice
among a clientele that was mostly Mormon, I can remember of
no instances in which I called the President of the Relief Society
and reported a family in need that there wasn't a gang of members there in a couple of hours, doing their best to straighten
out the tangle and put this unit of society back upon its feet
again. The church maintained a storehouse of foods and household necessities, and it made no difference whether the suffering
family was of Mormon faith or one of the myriads of other religious sects that might drift into a metal manufacturing town.
These ladies came with their baskets loaded with the things I
had reported lacking and when I got back the place showed the
results of a good cleaning and the emergency relieved.

My wife suffered from a multitude of nice old self-appointed
mothers-in-law, all of them good old Relief Society members
who took a motherly interest in her husband. But even they
were women, and upon occasion got out their hammers and gos-
siped a bit when a quilting bee was in progress.

I was once the subject of such a gathering, and I got a lot
more fun out of it than they did. One snowy evening I stopped
at the drug store to replenish my morphine supply, and as I was
leaving a young widow came in on her way home from work.
As she lived a mile from the store and as I was going next door
to her home on a call, I suggested that she climb into my car and
ride through the storm rather than walk so far facing that bliz-
zard. When we got to my destination she got out and went to
her own house, and I went in to relieve my patient.

A neighbor lady saw us get out of the car and quickly reported to the quilting gang that I was stepping out with the widow and was ashamed to drive up to her door. I heard about it the next day from one of my real female well wishers. When the ladies came around asking me to buy some chances on the quilt they were raffling off at ten cents per ticket, I only bought one instead of the customary fistful. I advised them that my reason was because they had talked about me while making the thing.

I won their old thirty dollar quilt for a single ten cent ticket, and I kept the thing and didn't give them any more money for it. That was the one time I was sore at the Relief Society. They had questioned the good name of a nice lady, and all she got from the "affair" was a mile ride through a snowstorm. As for myself, I didn't care what they said about me as long as I was innocent of the charges, but my self-esteem suffered considerably. I felt, I guess, much as would a successful retired bank robber who was accused of stealing from the collection plate in church. Even in my most coltish days I was better able to avoid "the appearance of evil" than that.

Those Mormon women were not perfect—who is?—but they did more good in less time and with less fanfare and fuss than any organization I was ever acquainted with.

In the course of thirty years of medical practice and another ten as member of state and county health boards, I have known a lot of social workers, investigators, public health nurses and all the other women connected with handling of the poor and unfortunate, and I would rather have twenty nice old Mormon Relief Society workers than the lot of them. There was nothing legal or confining about their approach to problems of a neglectful mother or a drunken bum of a father. They dressed him or her down like first sergeants bawling out awkward squads, but without cussing or shouting. And they caused the erring one to mend his ways, or else.

Of course legislative action is the only way to handle these situations at the state and national level, but the Mormons accomplished the same results with the expenditure of little or no money, and did the job because their society leaders assigned the task to them. They took the Lord's admonition "If you love me, feed my sheep" in dead earnest. Though individually they had as many female traits and exasperating habits as any other women, when they went on Relief Society business they accomplished their mission with efficiency and dispatch.

It may or may not be of any significance that this faith is founded upon the idea that the male shall be the head of the house, both in domestic and community projects, as well as in religious procedures. I'm not saying that he always qualified in the domestic situation—far from it. But outside the home the Mormon ladies took orders from their church leaders with little or no shirking.

In the lecture quoted in the first chapter, the old doctor said women would be governed by the demands made upon them by their ovaries for the first fifty years, and he might well have included for the rest of their lives. Though the ovaries cease to function in the decade we are describing, their influence carries on to the end. After the menopause a woman is still a woman except for her inability to bear children; this lack makes her even more unstable an organism, as she now has no ultimate objective.

But beware! There is another pitfall ever likely at this time in a woman's life—the arrival of another child long after the baby cribs and such have been sold to the secondhand dealer. And here, because of an early experience, I am of a superstitious nature. Our oldest boy was eighteen months old and my wife was convinced that she would never need the baby buggy again, so she sold it to a friend. The next month she was trying to buy it back. It so happened that we had not disposed of the crib; we kept that thing knocking around the storeroom until last week when we gave it to the Goodwill wagon. (My age being seventy-five and hers sixty-seven we felt that we were not taking too big a chance in disposing of it at this time.)

Humans, like plants, seem to anticipate the date of a killing frost and rush to maturity. As the days grow shorter the female reproductive system makes one last heroic effort before the frost of time catches up with it, and precautions that were adequate for years fail you at this late date. This failure is sometimes the result of planning by the mother, because the thought of no more babies frightens a woman of forty more than the changes in her own physiology. However, if she is not involved in the accident you are in the doghouse for the ensuing months. Now is a good time to join the Army or take passage on a moon rocket; whatever you meet will be a welcome relief from the domestic atmosphere at home.

So if your wife fails to menstruate for three or four months and decides that everything is over, you may both get careless, and "Bang!" Those little sex glands, in one last despairing effort, have produced another egg, and it has set up housekeeping. There are some few women who consider this a gift from on High, but most of them consider it an abomination from the devil, and to them you and Satan are one and the same.

Under certain circumstances, you and Satan are one and the same.

I well remember one kindly old lady who came into the office one day to engage my associate for a confinement case. The doctor was naturally suspicious of the abdominal swelling and called me in to examine her along with him. We were convinced that she had an enormous cyst in her abdomen, a diagnosis that was proved correct next day on the operating table. But when the doctor informed her that the supposed baby was a sack of water she burst into tears.

"What's the matter?" he said. "Did you want another baby at your age?"

"Oh no," she replied, "I'm happy about your conclusions, but I'm crying for poor Harry. I haven't spoken a kind word to him in three months!"

A doctor is of necessity mixed up in these domestic crises that occur at this time of a woman's life, and they are more tiring and time consuming than any other thing connected with the practice of medicine. One can do little to relieve them as time is the best medicine. The estrogenic compounds may relieve the symptoms for the time being, but they only seem to delay the ultimate conclusion, so they are much like cutting off the little dog's tail a bit at a time so it won't hurt so much.

In a man the experiences would be hilarious, but they are so real and of such consequence to the female sex that even the doctor can see nothing funny about them. To a woman, life is real and life is earnest because, as I have stated before, she is born grown-up and never will be able to appreciate the lacka-daisical manner in which her mate travels through this vale of tears. He, unfortunately, never grows up, and though he may ac-quire the appearance of reason and decision, just underneath the skin remains the little boy whose wild imagination and lust for the fun in life may take over at any moment. This is the principal gulf between the sexes: man's idiotic sense of humor pitted against a seriousness and purpose in his mate. These forces balance each other in the long run, but there are many wild dips of the needle on the scales before the partners both get too old to care a damn.

You pledged to love, honor and cherish her, and now is one of the times that you may regret that pledge, but stay with it, buddy. If she is a real woman there is far more happiness in store for you in the *next* twenty-five years than you had in the *last* twenty-five. Remember what the old doctor said: "She is a gift from the Lord, with a gentle assist from the devil, and she just cannot help some of the devil's inheritances cropping up on occasion."

13

Getting Through the Gloomy Fifties

And why with you, my love, my lord,
Am I spectacularly bored,
Yet do you up and leave me—then
I scream to have you back again?
DOROTHY PARKER

I F THERE IS such a thing as the so-called "moment of truth" in the life of a woman, it is the day she reaches her fiftieth birthday. One life is behind her; that for which she was trained from the cradle is now just a memory. There are another twenty-five years or so still ahead, but from the fiftieth milestone they may look bleak indeed. She is the same woman, but the allure that she so cherished is definitely on the wane.

Struggle as she may to appear years younger and more glamorous than she did at thirty-five, she finds that she must cherish the admiring male glances because there are greater intervals between them. And even when she does seem to attract the attention of a male, she is left in doubt as to whether he is just trying to sell her some gilt-edged real estate in Florida that is still populated by alligators. And most horrid thought of all, perhaps he is simply laughing at her makeup and youthful dress.

If she is alone and searching for a mate, she finds that her brain is dictating her actions rather than her heart. She would much prefer a bank account to the most ardent male, and she finds herself wondering if he snores and leaves his artificial dentures in the bathroom except when company is expected.

If there is a moment of truth, it is the day she reaches her fiftieth birthday.

There is no greater obstacle to true love than false teeth sitting in the Polident rather than where they belong. On the other hand there is no feeling so comfortable and satisfactory as admiring one's private jewels from afar. I spend a good deal of my waking hours in a little office adjoining my garage, and the first thing I do when I get there is to install these ornaments on top of a filing cabinet where I can look up from my writing and be greeted by their assuring grin. Writing about people is bound to make one somewhat blue and disheartened, but their ever-cheerful leer restores my natural sunny disposition, the world looks more like a joke, and I realize that things just cannot be as bad as they appear.

However, I have known some women who had this awful habit and I know of nothing that would make a man so long for bachelorhood and restaurant meals. Artificial dentures are often much more attractive than a woman's natural teeth, and if kept in their proper place are no hindrance to romance. In fact I have often thought they might be an aid to feminine beauty; they would, for a time at least, deter the female from loading up so heavily with foods. At the age of fifty, extra calories make their presence known by too many unsightly bulges in the wrong places. Anything that would restrict a female's appetite at this age improves the scenery.

Fifty is an age of trial and frustration for the woman who was not born with a compulsion to become a homemaker and a caretaker for one of the opposite sex. Unless a woman in this age bracket has a lot of household chores that must be done she is in the same sad fix that upsets her husband at sixty-five: nothing to do and the rest of her life to do it in.

The man usually solves this problem by curling up and dying; fifty per cent of retired men pass on within two years after they stop working. But the female is made of sterner stuff, and no woman has ever died just because she was bored with the business of living. She just wasn't made that way and has to cling to life until the last bit of vital force has drained from her body. So what is she going to do with the next thirty years? She has outgrown the P.T.A. and Camp Fire Girls, and if she has not succeeded in reaching the upper brackets of the pecking order in other do-good societies she is tired and disillusioned with the work connected with them. She is bored, often literally to tears.

Boredom is an awful handicap to peaceful co-existence in married life; a wife who is bored is often a problem of more importance than the state of your business affairs. *Newsweek* recently carried a summary of an address given by a New York psychiatrist on this subject, and I think the good doctor had females in mind when he spoke. The article reads as follows:

"Dr. Martin scoffed at the notion that people will eventually learn to handle free time by themselves. Psychiatry, he said, must find a way to give them a helping hand. Otherwise, he warned, in the automated life of the future with its promise of great leisure, human beings may become sterile robots, alienated from life and from themselves, living vicariously and so deadened that they compulsively seek overstimulation from the extreme, the lurid, the bizarre and the macabre."

With all this leisure the woman of fifty may seek her stimulation from romance, but she soon finds that this is something she can only enjoy vicariously by reading the best sellers. Lurid and bizarre romance are available here by the truckload.

I once asked an old and wise physician why women in this age group seemed to revel in novels where the author tried manfully to incorporate more different kinds of rape in his tale than did the last best seller. His answer was short and blunt: "Just trying to find out what they missed in life!" If women enjoy this second-hand dirt as much as boys enjoy lingerie advertisements and naughty postcards they should be forgiven because of their retarded adolescence. But there should be a law prohibiting them from discussing such books and claiming to understand that the underlying motivation of the author was to show that life can be beautiful. His real motivation was royalty checks from the publisher.

After romance is gone and her productive sex life is finished, woman starts out with renewed vigor in search of her female personality. She craves that illusive spot in the sun, but once she finds it all she gets is sunburn.

Woman has always required some activity for her hands. She cannot sit in the sun and read all the time, but she has lost her mother's talent with knitting needles and crochet hooks because she can now buy at the ten cent store better lace than she can make. Needle point is still slightly fashionable, and if worse comes to worse she can make a hooked rug. But most women have substituted the cigarette and the cocktail glass for the needles and hooks that used to keep their hands occupied.

This woman is the ultimate tragedy of our so-called advanced civilization. Man is taught from the cradle that his principal mission in life is to provide for his family; the kids grow up and get out on their own and now father's only responsibility is to accumulate enough money so mother can live in comfort and ease for the rest of their journey together, *and* for the long and useless years after he has passed from the scene. This thing never bothered our grandpas or our fathers. At fifty our mothers were as busy as at thirty, but times have changed.

In the old days women began their breakfast preparations in the evening, putting the oatmeal in the double boiler and letting it cook for a few hours before the kitchen fire went out, and setting the starter for the hotcakes. But what does the modern wife do if she gets up at all before her man goes to work? She dumps a spoonful of instant coffee into his cup, sets the package of prepared cereal and a carton of milk on the table, drops a slice of bread into the toaster, collapses on a chair, lights up a cigarette, and then returns to bed, growling because she has a man of such small attainments in the breakfast-getting arts.

She dumps a spoonful of instant coffee into his cup.

When she does get up, she dumps the remains of the repast into the garbage disposal, jams the dishes into the dishwasher and the dirty clothes into the washer-dryer, presses a few buttons, and turns on a few switches. Then there is nothing to do until mid-afternoon when she drives a block to the supermarket to pick up some frozen dinners, instant mashed potatoes and cottage cheese for a salad. Fifteen minutes before hubby is due home from the office she turns on the electric stove, heats the dinner, sets out the cocktail makings, lights the candles on the dining table, gives her fingernails a fresh coat of paint, and is all ready to go out for a night on the town when papa has finished his dinner. What if he *is* tired and frayed from a hard day at the office? All the books say this is the way to entertain your man. Besides, the quicker she can wear him down to the point where he will have a heart attack, the quicker she will come into his insurance and not have to bother with a man around the house.

What did her grandmother do after breakfast? She washed the dishes, set a baking of bread, washed out the clothes on a board that required more up and down motions of her back muscles than eighteen holes of golf, ran them through a hand-turned wringer, peeled spuds, shelled peas, cut meat and worked like the devil to get lunch ready on time as her man was likely to be home for this "dinner," which in those days occurred at twelve o'clock sharp. In the afternoon, she amused herself darning, sewing on buttons and, because there was no drip-dry in those days, put the big heavy irons on the stove to heat and ironed half a dozen clean shirts for her man and boys to wear the next day. By that time it was time to think about what she would serve for supper.

During her spare hours in summer she canned fruit, and in winter she went to a meeting of the society for foreign missions and sewed for the heathen.

Granted that when bedtime came this woman of days gone by was tired and weary, she nevertheless had the satisfaction of knowing that she had baked the best batch of bread her male dependents would ever eat, by her own efforts she had largely clothed them, and by both word and example she had done what she could to make them better citizens and a credit to her upbringing.

Instead of worrying ourselves sick trying to get a man on the moon before the Russians do, we should look at some other aspects of their culture. Mature females in Russia command ships, collective farms, and God knows what all. But at least the Russians are keeping their women busy.

The current American female, if she has a husband who is at all successful, cannot go out and get a job in industry without the finger of scorn being pointed at her for forcing some man out of a job. The husband's prestige is lost because his wife works, and consequently the stock in his company goes down on the New York Exchange. So she is condemned to a life as useless and worthless as that of the poodle that she leads around on a chain. Her hair is cut in the style of that same poodle and dyed, like as not to blend with the dog; they both may be sporting a new purple tinting job. Her eyelids, thanks to the new cosmetics, are a complementary color to her gown—blue today, green tomorrow, and lavender on Saturday night. Her face is covered with makeup, her neck encased in a collar similar to the dog's, her gown anything that a crazy Frenchman may dream up and which bears no relation to comfort or attractiveness, her legs as near bare as is possible, her feet propped up on heels three inches high with a walking surface smaller than a dime.

Her days are spent in bridge parties, cocktail swilling and fashion shows; her nights in more bridge, cocktails and dining at a dump which hides its cheapness by candle light, so noisy with floor shows that conversation is impossible. And so to bed. Tomorow is another day just like the one just past except that "Queen for a Day," "Life Can Be Beautiful" and "Can this Marriage Be Saved," will be on the TV program, so she will skip the afternoon bridge.

Her husband long since turned to some chick for love and companionship, her children and grandchildren need her about as much as another hole in their heads, her girdle hurts and her feet ditto. Just why *should* she get up in the morning? But underneath it all is as tough and resilient an organism as was ever turned out by an all-wise creator. She is healthy as a bear and has an appetite like one. Yet her only possible break from the monotony is that dearest of feminine dreams, some new and interesting ailment. If she can hatch one up which will

cause her to fade away in a most theatrical manner, she will at
long last satisfy her eternal longing to be the heroine in tragic
scenes such as the great Bernhardt used to play. So she skips
the Friday bridge games and goes down to tell her troubles to
her medical adviser—only, of course, if there is no possibility of
her having anything wrong.

From the beginning of time when Cain captured the Nod
maiden, woman has used her apparent helplessness to control
the big brute she married and her favorite means was and is to
complain of illness. I have known more than a few families
whose every action was goverened by mother's weak heart, and
after father had been long gathered to his reward and the children established in homes of their own (close to mother by the
way, that they might be handy to shield her from harm), that
old heart was ticking along as regular and as strong as a shock-
proof watch.

In an eariler day women resorted to hysterical fits to gain
their ends. They were so common that when my wife would
answer the phone and hear a frantic voice asking that the doctor come quick because Mrs. Blank was numb all over and
seemed to be dying, her stock reaction was to say, "Give her
the smelling salts, rub her wrists with alcohol and I'll tell him
when he comes in," and then promptly forget all about it. She
used to cuss and wish that she had never married a doctor because the others girls seemed to have so much fun having fits,
and she was afraid to try it for fear of a spanking. That fear was
enough; I was never driven to violent measures of any kind in
our domestic relations, but I have seen plenty of other cases
when they seemed justified.

I often think that spankings, either for the patient or her family, are the best possible prescription for many feminine ail-
ments. I once lost the practice of a very good family because I
would not tell a husband that it was necessary for his wife's
health that she be sent to southern California for the winter.
Her cousin had moved there from the East and was having such
a good time that she wanted the lady to come down and enjoy
it with her. She went, so I suppose some other doctor was more

obliging than I was in that case, but she ought to have been spanked instead.

Another time a young married woman came to me and wanted to borrow a book on physical diagnosis. When I asked what she wanted of it, she said she intended to have a heart attack. They were living with his folks and she decided that if she had a heart attack she could persuade hubby to move to a home of their own. I knew her mother-in-law and had a lot of sympathy for the girl, so I offered to coach her in the act, providing she would call some other doctor at the fatal moment. I knew I would be liable to laugh when I saw the real performance. She agreed, and within an hour I had her so letter perfect that any physician, without a cardiograph tracing, would have diagnosed a coronary.

It all worked out as planned except that once she got away from the in-laws her recovery was astounding, and the other doctor got the credit for great therapeutic skill in the treatment of this disease.

The girl who wanted to go to California was using unfair means to accomplish her desires and should have known that no husband would join her in the deception of another of the clan unless he was pretty much feminine in his makeup. My only excuse for my actions in the case of the girl suffering from too much in-law trouble was that I knew the in-laws and felt that this was the best way, short of a spanking, to get back at the old lady who was one of my most severe critics. I did try to convince the girl that a better way to handle the situation would be for me to talk to her husband and try to show him the impossibilities of domestic harmony under the existing circumstances. These situations were handled in a truly feminine manner, which is definitely a mystery to the male, unless he happens to be an old family doctor whose professional life was devoted mostly to dealing with women.

My female assistants always insisted that many women came to see their doctor for the same reason they went to the hairdresser or the beauty parlor. It wasn't as much fun as buying a new hat, but it was better than gabbing with the same old bags day in and day out over the bridge tables. Besides, it entailed the monopolizing of a male's undivided attention for a while, even if she did have to pay for it. It was better to have a man pawing about her anatomy, even with a stethoscope and rubber gloves, than to have no man and no pawing at all.

A doctor who cannot find something interesting to treat or give advice about is a poor stick and deserves to be unsuccessful in his practice. The gals must be amused, and it is remarkable how much conversation a woman can milk out of a simple diet list. A doctor who believes that he has done his duty when he tells his lady patient not to eat so much, and lets it go at that, is doomed to failure. Medicine is a wonderful profession, and the doctor who refuses to go along with the act and relieve the boredom of his mature female patient is an ass. She doesn't care, just so you find something that will be a subject for conversation at the bridge table. Tell her that her uterus is pointing northeast when it should be canting in a southwesterly direction, and she will leave the office as happy and content as a dog with two tails.

Because of the monthly evidence of activity in her generative organs, a woman looks upon this part of her anatomy much as an altar boy looks upon the sacred candles—as something that needs constant tinkering so it will give forth a clear and steady light. Consequently the average general physician spends more time in investigating and advising about this focal point than all other parts of the human body combined. In fact there is hardly a disease in woman, be it in her head or in her toes, that does not in some way lead back to this fountainhead of her life.

When I started to practice medicine it was believed that doctors should be able to find some pathological condition to explain every ache and pain complained of by the human race, otherwise we were a bunch of quacks. Time and experience taught me that women, and to an extent men, often complain of some bodily distress when the real cause of the trouble was all in their minds. My hard-won knowledge of earlier days is now universally accepted; *psychosomatic* is a fashionable word even at cocktail parties.

One little matron about drove me nuts trying to get me to convince her husband that her very life depended on her having another baby. By listening around to our mutual gossipy friends, I found that she wanted a baby because she thought it would distract hubby from his interest in his secretary. I told her there was no medical reason for her to insist on having another child, and that she would have to settle her domestic difficulties herself. That woman, who was as healthy as a bear, soon began to develop every symptom of every disease described in the medical columns of the ladies' magazines, and I think I suffered with those symptoms more than she did.

My star mistake in the treatment of the female occurred when I was young, brash, and full of ignorance. I had a lady patient who was sure that there was an elixir of life someplace, and she meant to find it. She consumed gallons of Lydia Pinkham's compound until she heard that there was a baby in every bottle (a rumor I sometimes wished were true), so she gave that up and called me, the new young doctor. I could find nothing whatever the matter with her and concluded, rightfully I think, that she was a simple hypochrondriac. But she just had to have a bottle of medicine. In desperation I took a bottle down to the old-fashioned drug store where there were rows and rows of large, square, glass-topped bottles along the walls, each of them bearing a gold-plated name in Latin on the outside, and some dried up junk on the inside that was about as inert and useless as pine chips. I put into my bottle a bit from every other bottle in that drug store and then for good measure I added some tincture of valerian, a drug which smelled so bad that the druggist always took it out behind the store before uncorking the bottle. I gave it to the lady at no charge, saying that the concoction was a new discovery I wanted to try out. She was delighted, and I heard no more from her. Then, about a month later, I got an agonized call from the druggist. The lady wanted him to refill the prescription, and he hadn't the faintest idea how to begin, and demanded that I come down and do it myself. I had made no record of the mixture, having expected the woman to throw it out the window as soon as she opened the bottle, and now I was stuck. She never forgave me or the druggist, believing that we were both conspiring with her husband to keep her in ill health.

Women for years depended on Prickly Ash Bitters, Lydia Pinkham and Peruna for their physical welfare. Now vitamins have largely displaced those harmless nostrums; the modern female dutifully stuffs herself and her family with ABCDEFG pills of all colors and sizes, thinking thereby to ward off the evil eye. The same reasoning prompted Grandpa to wear a bag of asafetida, a nasty smelling gum, to keep the germs away, but his conduct was more understandable—the smell kept people away, and people carry germs.

Of course there is a lot of hokum in this profession of doctoring as well as all the others, and ninety-five per cent of it is in connection with female patients. They have got to have something interesting wrong with them or they will hunt up a doctor who will find something. After all, bridge, hairdos, and gossip about other women's husbands will not fill the void left in the heads of women past fifty by being cut off from some useful accomplishments. It is up to us doctors to add some spice to a dreary existence.

But there is another side to the coin; some women are so considerate of others that they disregard their own troubles entirely. I told in another chapter of a picture bride from Japan. When this little lady had her first baby, I went to her home with my nurse to deliver it. We arrived in plenty of time, and as the girl was quite timid I instructed the nurse to keep her covered until our services were needed. My nurse sat by the bed and I retired to another room. The Japanese did everything they could to make a doctor's stay comfortable; there was an easy chair, and upon a stand beside it cigars, refreshments and the daily paper. After I had been settled for a while I heard the patient speak to the nurse in Japanese, went in and so I called the husband to come and interpret for us. He said, "She say excuse please, but she think it is nice baby." I threw back the sheet, and it certainly was a dandy baby. I asked the husband to ask her why she had not told us of the impending arrival of the baby, and after a quick exchange of words he replied, "She not like to bother nurse as nurse was reading book." I was amazed;

not a grunt or a groan simply because she didn't want to disturb anyone.

Another time I had to tell a woman the sad truth that she had an inoperable cancer. She swore me to secrecy because she said her husband would worry so, and she kept the information to herself until a week before she died. How she did it I'll never know and greater consideration for a husband's feelings I've never seen.

A doctor's life is made up of treating the most simple and the most complex of women, the brave ones and the cowards, the generous and the self-centered. It doesn't take him long to learn that woman is the most unpredicatable animal that walks the earth.

This chapter is not written with the idea of making disparaging cracks about elderly women. I love all of them; they paid my rent and fed me for thirty-five years. But I want to show just how badly civilization has treated them and what an impossible spot we have placed them in with our progress. Like the delinquent youngsters, there is nothing wrong with them that a little goal pointing and hard work will not cure. It's up to the male of the species to dream up some creative tasks for these bored and unhappy people. So I warn you, if you wish to avoid loss of face of such concern to our Chinese brothers, you had better worry more about the problem on your doorstep than the atomic bomb.

This decade known as the gloomy fifties is a difficult period in a woman's life. She is too old for romance, but not old enough to give up the struggle and settle down to a quiet old age. May I suggest, my dear brothers, that you forget the young chicks who try to make you forget your own age and spend a bit more thought on ways to make life more interesting for the aging filly who has pulled her share of the load over so many hills and rough roads in your journey together to this fateful spot.

14

Dear Old Souls— and Witches

There are three classes into which all elderly women that I ever knew were to be divided: first, that dear old soul; second, that old woman; third; that old witch.

SAMUEL TAYLOR COLERIDGE

BUT TIME GOES on and women do not have Joshua's knack of making the sun stand still, so they eventually reach the age of sixty-plus. This brings up a vexing and serious problem. For thirty years they have been hiding their birth certificates and subtracting anywhere from five to ten years from their true age. Now they try to erase all those past vanities; suddenly sixty-two becomes the desirable milestone.

Nothing on earth could make them confess the past deceptions, except the Social Security examiners. It would be most interesting to know how many times a week those gentlemen hear a stammering woman confess that she put a false age on her last marriage license application, just because she didn't want the new husband to know that she was older than he, or some such valid excuse. I can hardly imagine her adding onto her age, even for the chance to gyp Uncle Sam. But the fact that she has been compelled by law to tell the truth for once in her life in no way changes the nature of a woman.

Let's look at some of the different kinds of ladies, now that they have passed the all-important milestone and are in their sixties. First the maiden ladies. They are strong in their opinions, and critical of all mothers of little children. Now that they have been freed from bondage by Social Security, they set out to see the world, burdened with hot water bottles and a firm conviction that they are going to find civilization wanting in many important ways. They realize that they are of no importance to anyone except themselves, and they quickly become the most self-centered and selfish individuals that walk the earth.

Next, the female equivalent of the eternal sophomore. She has been married a half dozen times, and still believes that she can charm men by acting dumb and kittenish. It is to be hoped that her search for personality will eliminate her from the picture.

Next, the sophisticated dame who smokes like a chimney, drinks whenever there is some one to be astonished at her mannish mannerisms, swears freely but out of tune, and tries to engage every male she meets in a discussion of the hidden message in the latest best seller. Like the twenty-year-old male, she is ready to lay down somebody else's life for a new and hopeless cause, and probably is secretly writing a weird novel or play that will revolutionize mankind's approach to life.

Next, the spoiled brat, whose mission in life is to make her own way the most rose-strewn and easy path possible. Age does not change her one bit; even at eighty she is still trying to separate her male relations from their wives. She assumes a degree of helplessness when any of said males are around, and hoards her triumphs to her breast. Why the Almighty lets her clutter up the earth is a mystery, but He does, even until the age of one hundred.

And last but not least, that grand old woman to whom life has not been too kind. She still gets her happiness in doing things for others, regardless of the fact that her efforts are taken for granted and therefore seldom appreciated. To misquote Shakespeare, she is the "noblest work of God, the paragon of the animals." These fine ladies could be, if they were only allowed, the wonderful grandmothers every child and even some adults used to dream about.

Before it became fashionable for women to have their babies in the hospital, grandma's home was the favorite refuge for the pregnant wife. Here she not only got the professional care of doctor and visiting nurse, but the loving care of grandma herself, who was always ready and willing to walk junior when he felt in need of a stroll in the middle of the night.

But that time is long past. Today grandma knows nothing about caring for babies, and is politely so informed by her daughters. They don't need her and what's more don't want her. She is too full of old-fashioned notions about drinking, smoking and such newly acquired female pastimes.

I have heard some heated arguments in my time because grandma insisted that the baby be dressed with a flannel band about his belly to keep that most important region extra warm and so diminish the likelihood of colic. It was a benefit, no question about that, but modern woman has been taught that her child will be more healthy and sturdy if he is allowed to roll around with nothing on but a shirt and diaper.

Grandma believed in cooking cereal and mashing vegetables from the table to supplement baby's diet, instead of buying his food in cans similar to those which contain Fido's dinner. (The fact that in the hurry to drive the older kids to dancing school the cans sometimes get mixed does little damage. Junior will not begin barking and raising his leg every time he passes a lamp post.) But in the raising of the modern child grandma is as sadly out of date and useless as an old fashioned cradle that you rocked with your foot while your hands were busy shelling peas.

In a lifetime of work, both mental and physical, I have always found it better to do the hard and disagreeable tasks first, and save those I enjoy until the afternoon. As in eating, I save the dessert until the last. So I will discuss first the women in their sixties that I hate and keep those that I love for the dessert.

Several years ago there was an article in the *Saturday Evening Post* which told the story of a man's family which was being slowly wrecked by his mother. Circumstances and her will forced him to keep her in his home. Finally things got into such a shape that he placed her in a rest home, even though the cost caused him and his family to make sacrifices of no small consequence. As a dutiful son he visited her regularly, and the tale of woe she poured into his ears was enough to cause a stone idol to weep. Finally, when he was about to go crazy, trying to decide whether to sacrifice his pleasant home and family relations or let his mother suffer, he told his troubles to the manager of the rest home. That lady advised him to bid his mother the usual tearful goodby after his next visit, and then hide and listen to what went on after he was supposed to have left. He hated to spy on his mother, but he was desperate.

The next week the old lady wept and moaned about how she had been cast off by her own child, and shed copious tears when he got up to leave. He walked out and hid behind a screen in the hall. Once she thought he was out of earshot, she came tripping down the hall calling cheerily, "Come on girls, I got rid of him at last. Let's start that bridge game all over again."

I do not remember the exact words, and I gave my copy of the magazine to the director of a local rest home, who enjoyed it mightily. At the time I was a member of the county health board and often made inspection trips to these rest homes. I was much surprised to find that many of them refused to have women patients at all, stating that a roster of males made a quiet and peaceful place, while the gentler sex made it seem as if a revolution were going on all the time.

Needless to say I am a firm believer in rest homes. Better that one person be lonely than that a whole family be made unhappy. There is no use to argue with these possessive mothers; arguing with a woman at any time is a waste of breath, and it is doubly so if she feels a proprietary interest in you or yours. I know that life for her is bound to be dull; that is, if she is willing to acknowledge that she is aged. It is not her fault, but her misfortune, that medicine has made so many strides in saving the elderly from death. She was constructed with such lasting

materials that it takes a lot to close her chapter. It is a perplexing problem to figure out what to do with her.

When you are confronted with the problem, insist that your
female relatives remain in their own homes as long as it is physically possible for them to do so. Lonesome they may be, but
they are far more happy there than any place else on earth.
When age and infirmities make this no longer feasible, mortgage
your house if necessary, and find a nice rest home for their remaining years. One mother-in-law can muddy up the limpid
stream of matrimony quicker and more thoroughly than a dozen
silly little vamps casting come-hither looks at the old man.

The woman who is fixed financially so that she needs no help
from her family is equally bored with her existence. In Salt Lake
City there was a nice apartment house close to a clinic with
which I was loosely associated. The doctors at the clinic insisted
that the place was full of doctors' widows, and each and every
one of them came over twice a week to have her blood pressure
taken. Having been doctors' wives, they were never asked to
pay for these services. The boys believed that it was some kind
of a game; the gal who had the highest reading won the day's
jackpot, or something of the kind.

And this brings up a point for husbands to think about. These
old gals are so homesick to have some male depending upon
them that they will fall for any good-looking youngster who
shows up looking for someone to aid him financially. They are
not overly generous with the young felines of their own sex,
but they will give their entire fortune to some sweet male who
appeals to their mother hunger so that he may start a Frosty
Shop among the Eskimos. Hardly a day passes that we don't
read about some kindly old lady becoming financially destitute
because, as she always says, "He was such a nice boy that I
lost my head." All women have this latent mother desire to
help the youthful males, but it is overpowering in the truly
feminine personality.

You may think you have discharged your obligations by taking care of your wife for forty years, but you are doing her a
disservice if you do not arrange for some trust company or
hard-headed businessman to keep a check upon her expendi-
tures and investments after you are in your grave. She is a

woman, and being such is not governed by calm judgments; her important decisions are most often arrived at by impulse or that so-called female intuition. And believe me, I am not trying to sell female intuition short; during most of a woman's life it is probably better than mature male reasoning. But when she reaches the withered age of sixty-two the old intuitive process, like your prostate gland, isn't what it used to be.

Throughout most of the preceding chapters I have tried, as a gentleman should, to excuse woman for her shortcomings by showing her to be a victim of the civilization in which she lives. I almost feel that woman has been more sinned against than sinning.

But now, when her husband reaches sixty-five, we come to a period in the marriage relationship when she is at last relieved of the feeling of inferiority and takes her place as an equal partner. In most cases she makes a sorry spectacle of her newly acquired role. Like the newly emancipated in all history, she tends to become the dominant figure and is guilty of excesses which ill become her.

The day a man retires, he lays away the masculine horns which denoted the fact that he was the bread-winner and protector of the home. Unfortunately his mate too often grabs them up, and there is nothing quite so sad as a lady deer wearing antlers.

Here are three short quotes from the noted French writer, Miss deBeauvior:

"After the change of life, woman's feelings toward her husband resolve themselves into three classifications—friendship, indifference, and lastly hostility."

"Man is much more upset than woman when the mate dies in old age."

"If her aging husband dies, she bears the loss most cheerfully."

When hubby, due to his retirement, is no longer the rock upon which the marriage was founded, all three of these quotations take on a more serious meaning. It is the universal opinion, publicly expressed by all wives of retired men, that though retirement may be hard on the old man, it is infinitely more difficult for his wife. *She* hasn't retired, and is still fulfilling her obligation of feeding the brute, though not always without protest.

I first came face to face with this change in status while quite a young physician. I was occasionally called to a nearby town to see an old man. Although his wife and even the dog usually slept in the house, more often than not I found *him* living in a little shack in the back yard doing his own cooking. The situation reminded me of Riley's poem, *Milo Jones' Wife*:

> Dad-burn Milo Jones' wife;
> Ruther rake a blamed case-knife
> 'Cross my wizzen than to see
> Sich a woman rulin' me.

The old man chose the cabin so he might have a little peace and quiet. He gave me a piece of advice spoken with the voice of experience: "Never leave your pants around where your wife can slip into them. If necessary wear them to bed and remember that it's more necessary at eighty than at twenty."

Never leave your pants around where your wife can slip into them.

I haven't followed his advice literally, but though I retired from my profession at sixty there hasn't been a minute in the following fifteen years that I wasn't positively wearing the pants and gainfully employed at something. I've spent ten years farming, and though my financial returns were small, still I brought in the milk and vegetables and so never lost my status as the provider. I am married to the best woman in the world, but I don't intend to give her the opportunity to look at me in that "what-the-hell-am-I-going-to-do-with-you" manner.

Since my own retirement, and the publication of my writings on the subject, I have had a wonderful opportunity to observe other men and their wives in retirement. At least a thousand elderly couples have called at my little farm seeking advice on this retirement question, and though I gave them the best advice I could, I got a lot more information out of the interviews than they did. More often than not, the slacks worn by the old lady out-shown the pants covering the man's knobby knees.

One old man was a kindly appearing chap about six feet, four inches tall, much bent with the load of years he was carrying. Now that he and his wife were retired and had enough money to see them through, he longed to settle up in the hills where he could be close to nature's heart, do a bit of fishing and bird watching, and try and forget the long years he had spent in the concrete jungles of a big city. The old lady was a sparrow type of female who ran on like a tape recorded in high gear, coming to the point quickly:

"Now my husband has the ridiculous idea that he would like to live up at the little settlement of Dutch Flats, and I have agreed to spend a month there just to humor him but I definitely will not consent to buying a home there, and just look at him, Doctor, and tell him the absolute truth. Do you think he has any chance of living more than a year or two to enjoy his silly wilderness ideas? Why there are no supermarkets and not even a good beauty parlor within miles of the place and I wouldn't stay there overnight except to show him that this nature-boy stuff is all hooey; we will live down on the coast of southern California so when I am left a widow I can have a pleasant home close to civilization and I just brought him up here for you to pound some sense into his head."

Her summation sounded as though she was discussing an old tree rather than her loving husband of forty years. I felt like suggesting that I get the axe and chop him down right now, before he got caught in a high wind and blew over on some-body. But being an old hand at such family arguments, I was most noncommittal in my answers. They didn't get to Dutch Flats; the poor old boy spent his remaining years looking at sea gulls and doing his fishing in an apartment, reading *Field & Stream.*

I do not know how long it was before he fell, but I do know that that man had a right to spend the years remaining to him as he saw fit. He had spent his life accumulating plenty of money so his old lady could live in luxury during her years of widowhood. And she wasn't kind enough to allow him this realization of a dream because she didn't want the bother of moving after he was gone. That picture is not overdrawn one bit, and if it weren't so monotonous I could fill this book with hundreds of similar instances.

Most of the harpies were second wives. They would drive up here as if the other passenger was an old and decrepit dog that had to be brought along. Hubby was not even allowed to touch the wheel of the car. She told him where to sit, how to smoke, where to deposit the ashes, and did everything but hold a handkerchief for him to blow his nose. My wife was dumb-founded the first few times she saw these performances, and it took her a while to control her giggles. But to me it was a familiar story.

A few months ago an elderly couple visited us. The old man revealed that he had been an officer in a large eastern banking institution, and that his first wife had died five years ago. We got to talking about the East, and I mentioned a neighborhood in a certain community there, saying that the residents were as trashy a bunch of people as any I'd ever seen.

"Yes sir," the old man spoke up, "you're dead right. That's where my wife hails from." And in the next breath he answered her summons with, "Yes, dear, I'm coming."

I am confident that that man will soon join his first wife on the other shore of the River Styx, just to get away from the hell his second wife is giving him on this side.

Too often it seems that these women value their husbands in direct ratio to the number of dollars they brought home; once the old man had finished his fruitful period in the financial world, they consider him a nuisance. And there is no time in life when a man so needs the comforting that only an understanding partner can give.

A man left a widower after the age of fifty is a poor confused child in sex relationships, and will be caught by the first woman who puts forth much of an effort. And believe you me these dames who have lost one husband (who probably died in self defense) are the babies who can put on the pressure when a comfortable bank account is in sight. There is no animal known that will hunt the unattached male of the species with the avidity shown by the aged female, and probably no animal as easily caught as an old widower. The old bachelor is a much more canny individual and is not pursued with much hope of success. But how the aging gals do whet up their teeth, camouflage themselves to blend with the surrounding scenery, and lurk beside the game trails when a widower is known to be in the neighborhood. This kind of hunting is closely related to dynamiting fish or shooting tame ducks on the pond, but it does put meat in the stew.

Younger women of a mercenary disposition are known to join in this badger game, but only if the quarry is pretty well encrusted with gold and if the hunting of more suitable game is poor indeed. The old arthritic female is not so particular; any kind of a dilapidated specimen is game, providing other aging females are on his trail.

I have spent forty years watching this cat and mouse performance, and it has made me thankful that my own wife seems to be of a lasting nature, because no man seems to be immune once his home has been broken up by death or divorce. One would expect Twentieth Century man to be the equal of the old Blackfoot Indian philosopher, who said: "White man fool Indian once—damn white man; white man fool Indian twice— damn Indian." But I have known men who have been fooled by predatory females four or five times.

The whole thing is based upon the differences inherent in the two sexes. When she is young, the female craves a home, but the male is inclined to wander and is restrained with more or less difficulty by his nesting mate. Once old age creeps up on them, the man desires his fireside rocking chair and a more settled existence. His mate, meanwhile, tries frantically to rid herself of such boring occupations as keeping house and catering to an old relic whose idea of fun is to watch the young women on TV and cuss the government.

Once old Father Time cuts him down, she bounces around like a chicken that has just lost its head. She takes a trip to Europe or the Islands and returns home full of the sights and experiences enjoyed by "Us Girls." Six months later she is to be found all togged out in her hunting clothes, with her bow and arrow at the ready, skulking around the Happiness Clubs in search of some poor defenseless old widower. And all so that she may once again have something to bitch about.

But how they do moan when the hunting is a bit poor. One discouraged widow confided to my wife and myself that if she could just have a man to get breakfast for she would be happy. We had known her *when,* and she was not home enough of the time to *think* about getting breakfast for her tribe. My better half, a lady who often speaks her mind, remarked, "Well, that would be a novel experience, wouldn't it?" The old widow is still on the prowl, all the uplift movements and suffering heathens of her earlier life forgotten in her quest for the ultimate joy of getting breakfast for some man. The man that falls for her had better know how to cook, because she will forget her longings once she has him for her very own.

There are a lot of do's and don'ts that the old widower should consider. I will list a few that observation has taught me, though I don't for a minute expect any old buck to remember them when the time of need arrives.

First get that silly idea out of your head that she is in love with you. A man of sixty, seventy, or even eighty, still believes himself to be the answer to a maiden's prayer. He is as full of puppy love as he was at sixteen, and consequently thinks that he is marrying for everlasting love just as he did the first time; all the evidences to the contrary are washed from his mind. The truth is that women are incapable of romantic love after the age of forty-five, and most of them reach that stage twenty years sooner. She wants to marry you for money—a home—or just to have something live about the house bigger than a love bird (they won't allow dogs in the apartment house where she lives).

Forget her protestations of passion. I have described one of these eager wenches in another chapter, but one more example will not be amiss. I knew a man who was in love, and how he was in love. He told me that they were perfectly matched; he was a he-man from away back, and she was a wonderful example of feminine passion and love. They got married, and within thirty days she explained to him that she had a fibroid uterus and would have to have an operation which would put an end to all his romantic dreams. He was forever afterwards a sour old goat who looked at the world through jaundiced eyes. It is better, however, that you don't get a sex kitten, because late activity along that line often seems to cause the male to pass out of the picture with a cancerous prostate.

Remember that you are the quarry and don't be too hasty in allowing yourself to be captured. You can stand restaurant meals for a few months longer; spend the time investigating the huntress with the full understanding that the female is not always what she seems at first meeting.

Drop in to visit about mealtime without announcing your coming; you should be able to recognize frozen dinners by this time.

Take her on a picnic on which you furnish only the transportation and the beer. If she brings out a bunch of cute little sandwiches cut to resemble hearts and flowers, with nothing in them but a lettuce leaf and a bit of liverwurst the size of a dime, think about that instead of her pretty ankles (encased in elastic stockings). If the lunch contains sandwiches with a big slice of beef, homemade potato salad, and a pie that shows no evidence of ever having been frozen, your future looks much better and you can go back to the ankles.

Notice her apartment. If it is a bit messy you can expect no fireworks when you spill ashes on the rug; but avoid the careful housekeeper who is always handing you ashtrays when you come to call. After she gets you, she will insist that you empty and wash your ashtray after every smoke. I have even known women who made their second husbands go to the basement for every puff of a pipe or cigarette.

Does she talk all the time when you are together? After you are married she will continue in that infuriating habit, and never give you a chance to express an opinion.

Does she have four or five lazy tomcats occupying all the easy chairs in the living room, or perhaps a fat wheezy dog or two? Such things can be irritating if you are not a lover of these useless decorations, and many a man has found himself playing second fiddle to a cat.

Suggest that you visit her children before you get too serious or make any wild promises. "By their fruits ye shall know them." A good woman will have good offspring, and you should be competent to judge at least the males; from their behavior you can learn a lot about your intended life partner.

Visit the widow's children before you make any wild promises.

The last admonition is the most important of all, and though I am not a lawyer I do know how it works. The state considers the female a second-class citizen, unable to look out for herself once she writes "Mrs." before her name. When you say "I do," you contract with the commonwealth to care for and cherish this lesser individual. Be you eighty years old and confined to a wheel chair, with a bride fair, fat, and forty and able to whip her weight in wildcats, once you are married your state looks upon *you* to be the sturdy oak and *she* the clinging vine. These ancient females all know about that provision on the legal code, and what they don't know some attorney will be happy to tell them.

Suppose you have a thousand or two saved up to assure of a decent burial for yourself. If she hears about it, no matter how well endowed with worldly goods she may be, she is going to demand that you spend that poor little nest egg for her upkeep and pleasure. If you refuse, prepare to meet her attorney. Non-support is a big tent under which many tricks are quartered.

You had better see your own attorney before taking the fatal step of proposing. I happen to know of one old gentleman who had some property in the East. Soon after he was married the second time, his new wife coaxed him to dispose of same and invest the proceeds in a larger house in a community property state. Once they were settled in the new home two of her married children brought their families to live with her, and the old man was forced to sleep in the kitchen. The house was full of so much confusion that finally he moved out. Now he lives the life of a hermit up in the mountains, existing upon his social security check. The second wife is living in a thirty thousand dollar home bought with his money, but I understand she sends him a greeting card every Christmas—a kindly gesture, I'm sure.

One more warning: Don't brag to her about your financial standing; there is no scorn like a woman's when she finds out hubby is not the old moneybags he pretended to be.

Get married by all means; a man of many years happiness in that state cannot live otherwise. But remember, you are not dealing with a trusting young female as was the case the first time, but most likely with a hard-bitten, worldly-wise, old sister who is looking out for herself, and herself alone. So make haste slowly, and look a long time before you leap into something for which your experience has not prepared you.

The jungle through which the widower must travel is badly

infested with big cats, most of them searching for companionship and a good life beside some domestic fireplace. But there
are also many of the man-eating variety in disguise; you can
usually tell them because they purr so much more readily and
with a lot more finesse.

I have neglected the women who have a feeling of friendship
for their elderly mates, because they are much more scarce. But
there is this other class of women who miss the companionship
and feel lost without some male to watch over them. If you can
find one of these, grab her; she will not expect too much and is
more willing to give than is common with the sex. It is a heart
warming sight to see an elderly couple who, though the fires of
love have burned low, are still warmed by understanding, affection, and dependence upon each other.

Sometimes women advise me privately that they know papa
will be disappointed in his retirement pursuits, and that they
have made plans to meet that emergency. But they are willing
to go native in a big way for a time, so papa may attain his
heart's desire. Those women are all too few.

One reason I moved my wife to a new community and different climate when I retired from medicine was to avoid this
painful adjustment. She had never grown used to having me
away all day because my home was close enough to my office
so that I seldom missed coming home for lunch, but I realized
that having a man around the house with nothing much to do
would worry her greatly. Once we were newly located she was
so busy finding fault with my choice of location that she appreciated my presence as an audience for her growls of discontent.
She got used to the new situation in both categories at the same
time, so I was spared those calculating looks that most elderly
men must endure.

You have got to face it fellows: once your obligations connected with raising a family are completed and there are
enough of this world's goods accumulated to provide for the
extras not covered by the social security check, you are as useless around the home as your own nipples. The little woman
promised to love and honor you till death do you part, but with
a lot of women death seems most deliberate in its deliverance.

Once you are seventy-two and can work without being penalized by the social security regulations, life can be wonderful again, but the first seven years after that magic sixty-five are the hardest years of your entire married life. Seventy-two is worth waiting for.

15

Conclusion: Now There Was A Woman

The head of the woman is the man . . . but the woman is the crown of the man.
                    I Corinthians, II:3-7

Enigma thy name is woman. When one reflects upon her nature and tries to plot her future course, it is natural to call up the images of those females who over the years have been sweethearts, patients and friends. Strange as it may seem, in the silent parade that passes through one's recollections, over half the women I have known are as domestic as hens. They consider it their manifest destiny to be keeper of the home fires, raising their children to be God-fearing citizens. Once that is accomplished, they devote their entire energy to keeping the empty nest attractive to the father bird. Though his voice may be cracked and his plummage mostly moulted, they still keep up the pretense that his music is the sweetest, his appearance the most attractive, and that social security worm that he brings home the sweetest morsel of them all.

Once he has been shot down by time's unerring arrow, they spend the rest of their days searching for some animate thing which they can mother. It may be the neighbor's kids, a dog, other inmates of the rest home—just anything so long as they are not completely useless. They go their way quietly.

It is an old but true maxim that the squeaking wheel gets the grease, and so a wicked minority of the sex is dragging the rest along toward destruction, doing their best to change the time-tested relationship between the sexes.

So now we come to the dessert, that class of women who believe from childhood in the Biblical statement that it is more blessed to give than to receive, and who cling to that long-forgotten precept until their last breath. The world is well populated with these wonderful women, and memories of them are strewn with flowers in the minds of those lucky enough to know them. It has been my own good fortune to have known many such women, and I will briefly sketch a bit of their personalities to show my admiration and respect for woman at her finest.

Mrs. C. was a guest at one of the rest homes with which I was familiar. She was a heart case, had an oxygen apparatus beside her bed, and lived with the knowledge that she might be called to take the last trip at almost any time. To talk to her, one would never dream that she was aware of her condition. She was as cheerful and as full of plans as a sixteen-year-old girl, and was never so happy as when one of the other guests had some darning or button sewing to be done. I saw her the day before she passed on and she was busy darning the stockings of a guest who just hated to darn stockings. Life to her meant doing something for someone else; she did not ask or accept anything for her services.

Another kindly old lady, who had been a widow for thirty years, referred to her husband continually as though he had only passed yesterday. She spent her happiest days just traveling around to the places they had enjoyed together, and she looked forward to her passing, not because she expected any crown in Glory, but because she firmly believed she would be reunited with her husband for the rest of time.

But the greatest woman I ever knew was Aunt Jennie, a Mormon midwife. She was a large, well-upholstered individual of sixty-five when I first met her, a natural diagnostician and the possessor of the most refreshing sense of humor I ever saw in a woman. Life in a small desert community had not been easy for her. Her husband had died when her children were very young, and to support them she had gone to Salt Lake City and taken a course in midwifery at the leading hospital there.

I quickly learned that I could avoid many long and unnecessary trips to her community if I insisted that Aunt Jennie be called to look at the invalid and her findings phoned to me. Though she had no training in medicine except what she picked up from us doctors, and never read a medical journal in her life, she seemed to have a sixth sense which guided her in picking out the serious cases from the merely excitable ones.

One night she called me about one o'clock and said she was worried, and asked that I come down. She couldn't sleep, and saw no reason why I should either. She had been called to see a little boy who kept his parents awake crying about a pain in his ankle. They thought it rheumatism, and called Jennie to come and direct them in application of hot packs to relieve the pain. She felt the joint, and somehow discovered that the pain was in the bone rather than the joint itself. Though she had never seen a case of osteomyelitis, she knew that this was not ordinary rheumatism.

A hurried operation and drainage of the infected area made this case a minor affair, but many another man is walking around today with a badly crippled leg because some doctor treated him for rheumatism or growing pains when he was a child. I have often wondered if I would have had the gumption to recognize the condition if I had seen that boy first, before Jennie called my attention to the unusual symptoms. I have always been happy that Jennie was on the spot and that my diagnostic abilities, befuddled by a lack of sleep, were not tested too severely in that case.

Another time she called and stated that she was completely at sea and would I come down and see a suspected inflamed appendix. When I arrived I found a forty-year-old blonde with a most generously upholstered abdomen. The history didn't sound right, there was no rise in the white blood count, and I couldn't feel a thing in the abdomen. Before making a decision, I suggested to Jennie that we go out into the yard and have a consultation. The first words she said were, "What did that abdomen feel like to you?" I ducked that one, gave a non-committal answer, and asked how it felt to her. She snorted a most descriptive answer, "Like a big pan of bread dough that badly needs working down." I had never enjoyed the experience of kneading bread dough, but I knew just what she meant. The anxious family probably thought me crazy to be laughing at such a time. We advised the patient to forget her bellyache and to give her digestive tract a few days rest from over-indulgence. Jennie shared my distatste for people who had allowed themselves to become mountains by over-eating.

One time I sent Jennie on a confinement case with the understanding that I would remain close to my telephone if she felt the need for my services. Pretty soon she called. Her conversation was somewhat vague because she felt that doctors and nurses should act dignified at all times; even on the phone she wouldn't discuss any subject which she considered too delicate for laymen's ears. What she said was, "Read Genesis 38, verses 27 and 28, and then get here as fast as you can." I grabbed a Bible, read the reference, and set sail for her location. For those who do not know their Bible well enough, I will say that this is the first reference to difficult childbirth in the Good Book; it refers to twins with one of them in a transverse position, an impossible situation for delivery without the aid of an experienced physician.

Jennie and I managed the feat, and once the twins were safely in this world I looked them over carefully and mildly chided Jennie for her negligence in failing to tie a string upon the protruding hand which had caused her, like that other midwife so long ago, to make her diagnosis.

As usual Providence seemed to add even bigger crosses to the back that bears the burden. For two years before Jennie died, she was a helpless invalid and toward the last even her mind was gone. Surely there must be a heaven someplace for people who spend their lives in the service of their fellow man, without thought of glory or financial reward.

Many doctors of the time fought with these old midwives who were necessities of an earlier day when doctors were not available. But I never knew one of these grand ladies that didn't practice a brand of professional ethics that was many a cut above that common with us physicians. I worked with more than a dozen of them during my years of rural practice before trained nurses became available, and I loved every one of them as a son loves a kind and understanding mother.

Sometimes they made mistakes and sometimes they were the butt of youthful pranks that to me were truly funny. One night I was doing a home delivery. The midwife took the baby into the kitchen while I was caring for the mother, and proceeded to oil and dress him by the light from the grate of the kitchen stove. (There was only one working light in the home—a coal oil affair, and I needed that in my work.) She directed an older child to bring her the cooking oil, as there was no pure olive oil to be had, and proceeded to cover the babe with the contents of the can she received. Pretty soon she came in and asked me to come and look at the baby; she swore that it was the stickiest kid she had ever handled. I went, and took the lamp with me. She had plastered the baby with Karo syrup from head to toe and to make matters worse it was an Italian with a mop of hair instead of a bald-headed Swede. I thought we were going to need a sandblaster before we got that baby free of the stuff, and I was much worried about his tender skin, but it seemed to be just what was needed. He was as pink and rosy as any baby I ever saw.

Another time I dropped in to leave some instructions for a practical nurse down in southern Utah, and found her having tea with "John's other wife." They were laughing over a ghastly joke they had played upon their common husband many years ago. He had been dead for fifteen years, and it was to be hoped that his spirit was far enough away not to hear the conversation, or he would have fallen from grace immediately. He had

Jennie swore he was the stickiest kid she had ever handled.

married my nurse when they were very young, and taken her out to the ranch some distance from any habitation. She was lonesome and begged him to take another wife, which he refused to do. When she went into the settlement to deliver her first baby, she confided her troubles to her dearest friend and between them they decided to two-time the old boy. They started a rumor that hubby was going to take the friend as a second wife. When he arrived he was confronted with the job of either making good or being branded as a heel that would trifle with an innocent girl's affections. He resisted with all of his might, but what man could battle with two determined women? He went home with two wives, and they all lived happily ever after.

Like the reader, it was hard for me to believe this story, but there they were, slapping their knees and laughing about how they bested the old man. And one thing I did know: they actually had been plural wives of the same husband. It all happened nearly a century ago, and perhaps women were different in those days. I have reached a stage where I am not surprised at anything the fair sex decides to do.

When I look back at all of the human contacts I have made in a busy life, my eyes only grow dim when I think about those dear old ladies who so deserved the Biblical song of praise. "I was sick, and you comforted me."

In a former book I described what I thought was one real life scene that would have made a wonderful painting if anyone had been around to paint it. Some scenes are retained in the memory long after the event takes place. Old Matt and the baby in my book *What Next, Doctor Peck?* was one of them, and Aunt Jennie is the principal figure in this one. I can go through a gallery of old masters or the modern abstractionists like a whirlwind and only think about my aching feet because I care nothing for fat little angels, wooden madonnas or cyclones of color. But here is a painting I wish I owned. The location: the simple cabin of a poor Mormon homestead, the room bare of furniture except for an old wooden bed, Mrs. Whistler's rocking chair, and an open-front Franklin stove. The time: night. The people: the father holding a coal-oil lamp, the mother lying in the bed in the background, and Aunt Jennie sitting in the rocking chair with a naked new born baby girl on her lap (she always bathed and dressed them in this position, having great scorn for a woman who needed a table for the delicate task). Before her stand two little girls, dressed in their nighties, with bare feet and towsled hair, gazing in big-eyed wonder at the package the stork has just brought. The lamp and the reflections from the open fire bathe the whole scene in a soft yellow light with shadows flickering as the fire burns high and low. Three generations—the grey-haired old lady with her mouth full of safety pins, the anxious father and quiet mother, and those two little awe-struck girls staring at the new baby. How much greater a painting this would make than a couple of fat angels floating around over a lavishly dressed mother. It is the essence of all the good women and fine people in the world.

When friends begin to discuss a mutual acquaintance, they

usually take for granted his more admirable qualities and concentrate on his unusual and bizarre traits. Somehow he seems more human if his faults are added to the picture.

In writing books, as in other forms of entertainment or enlightenment, this becomes even more important because it is only the unusual that will attract and hold the attention of the audience. Not many books describe the average man or woman, his more or less uneventful life, or his ordinary down-to-earth thoughts. The picture must always be overdrawn.

Such has been the case in this book. I have ignored the hundreds of women who came to my office with ordinary problems; women who nevertheless have all the emotions, complexes and delusions of the sex. These women, because they are civilized human beings, have learned, in a great measure, to suppress their semi-savage natures so they may live at peace with themselves and their husbands.

Throughout most of the animal kingdom the female resents the attentions of the male except at the times when she needs his fertilizing powers; in many species the male is not allowed in the herd except at these times. So we know that there must be a bred-in animosity felt by the female sex in general toward their mates. The human female has learned to suppress this animosity for the greater good of the family, and she has, in most cases, done a wonderful job of it.

To understand the gentle and affectionate wife, we men must understand that many of her actions are the result of long training; to understand the scope of her accomplishment we must study her less inhibited sisters. No man knows what constitutes the normal mentality until he has studied the abnormal or exaggerated symptoms. None of us are very far from our cave man ancestors; we tend to relapse into their ways under stress, men more than women because men have had less training in self-discipline.

Each of us is a self-centered individual. We are born into this world alone, and we live and leave it in the same lonesome state. Be our life span long or short, our only hope of achieving a degree of fellowship is to so modify our personalities that we can live in close communion with some woman. It is fortunate

In many species the male is not always welcome in the herd.

for men that woman *is* of a different race and temperament; were she like us, we would all be bored sick before the ink on the marriage certificate was dry. It was a wise Providence that so arranged our personalities that they blend best with those of some female, and that the female personality is so flexible that she can adjust herself to the impossible conditions of living in harmony with the male.

No one enjoys the feeling of inferiority, but in order to make man function as his creator intended he should, woman has accepted second place. Granted that she is not too happy with the situation, but she is willing to put up with it to gain a degree of peace and harmony in the marriage relationship and to insure her offspring a pleasant environment. Such an unequal relationship is not ideal, but people were not put on earth to achieve the ideal—only to pursue it.

So I would advise you, my gentlemen friends: study woman as does an anthropologist, part by part, action by action, mood by mood, and perhaps you will eventually come up with some idea about just what makes your wife react the way she does.

And never, no never, take her for granted and expect her to see things from your viewpoint. You can live most happily with her for a lifetime if you will always remember that she is a different sort of an animal, created specially for a certain purpose, and that the easy companionship that may exist between males is forever impossible between you two. She is superior to you in most every way except brute force and long range thinking, more tender and yet more cruel, more yielding yet more determined, more innocent and yet more filled with guile, and firm in her belief that anything you can do, she can do better. And damn it, too often she is right.

But when all is said and done, man can echo the epitaph Mark Twain attributed to Adam after Eve's passing: "Wheresoever she was, *there* was Eden."

About the Author

Joseph Howard Peck, born in 1885 in Breckenridge, Missouri, is a fine example of what is generally thought to be a vanishing breed: the down-to-earth country doctor. Settling in the rugged desert country of Utah, he practiced there for over thirty years. At the age of sixty he and his wife Ruth, retired to a little farm in the foothills of the Sierra in Northern California. Like many a physician before him, he gave in to the urge to peck out his experiences and flinty philosophy on an antique portable. On a dare from Ruth, he sent the *Saturday Evening Post* a mellow piece about the pleasures and vexations of retirement. This resulted in a check for $850, a series of articles in the magazine, and a procession of envious visitors to the farm that has yet to cease. Warming to his new career, Dr. Peck next produced a remarkably original book, *All About Men*, published in 1958. An immediate bestseller, this trenchant manifesto delighted a legion of readers in America, was serialized to millions in several hundred newspapers and has been published widely abroad in numerous translations. *What Next, Dr. Peck?*, reminiscenses of the Utah years, appeared a year later and was widely praised as authentic Americana.